A GUIDE TO
AMERICAN FOOTBALL

A GUIDE TO
AMERICAN FOOTBALL

KEN THOMAS

With a foreword by Nicky Horne

Orbis Publishing, London

In association with
Channel Four Television Company Limited

I am indebted to Commissioner Pete Rozelle of the National Football League, who has freely provided a wealth of information; to John Bromley and his colleagues at World of Sport; Adrian Metcalfe, Head of Sport at Channel 4 Television and Cheerleader Productions Ltd., for their vision in pioneering American Football in the United Kingdom; to Nick Wridgway and Roger Smith for proof reading; and to my wife Janie, for yet another Football season of tolerance. To them all I offer my grateful thanks.

K.T., 1983

Printed in Great Britain
ISBN 0-85613-571-2

CONTENTS

FOREWORD

Well, at last, here it is. All you ever wanted to know about American Football in one handy volume. This is a book that I will be using myself to check all the complexities of this most fascinating game. For you to have bought this book means that you are already hooked on American Football and the following pages will give you an encyclopedic knowledge so that you can understand it far better and also impress your friends in the pub ... happy reading.

NICKY HORNE

INTRODUCTION

American Football is not unlike the codes of rugby football in that the ball is the same shape (prolate spheroid), the goal posts are similar and serve an identical purpose, and players attempt to make forward progress by running with the ball in hand. Furthermore, the principal method of halting the ball-carrier is by tackling. However, in American Football, once the ball-carrier is tackled to the ground, or clearly held, the ball is ruled dead and play comes to a complete halt. It restarts with a set piece, a face to face confrontation known formally as a 'Scrimmage' but idiomatically as a 'Down'. The team in possession is allowed four of these downs. By using one, two, three or all four downs, ten or more yards must be gained. If this yardage requirement is satisfied, possession is retained and a new set of four downs is earned. By repeatedly gaining the necessary ten yards within the sequence of the four downs, possession is maintained and the attacking team (known as the 'Offense') moves systematically down the field, with the eventual object of scoring. If the offense fails to make the necessary ten yards during a particular four-down series, possession is transferred to the opposition (formerly the 'Defense'), which then becomes the attacking team (offense) and embarks on its return drive. This then is the basis of the ebb and flow of American Football.

The game takes place on a pitch measuring 360 feet long and 160 feet wide (Fig 1). The choice of width was neither arbitrary nor ordained, but simply was the maximum available to Walter Camp

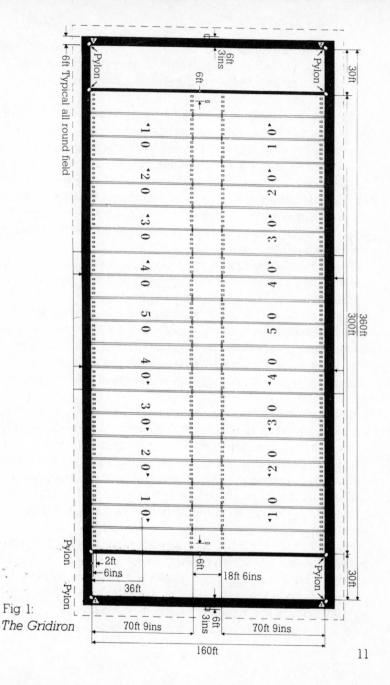

Fig 1:
The Gridiron

11

when he set out to formalize the game in the 1880s. It is essential and convenient that the pitch be marked out at intervals of 5 yards and, to a lesser extent, 1 yard. The pitch therefore has the appearance of a 'Gridiron', which has become a popular name for it.

The prime objective is to score a 'Touchdown', worth 6 points, following which there is a kick at goal worth 1 point, called 'Extra Point Attempt'. There is also the possibility of scoring with a 'Field Goal Kick' (3 points), which can be attempted at all times during the game on any set-piece down, and from any yardage position. The obvious comparison is with a penalty kick at goal in rugby, yet since an infringement by the opposition is *not* a prerequisite, more sensibly it might be compared with a drop kick at goal, which in rugby too forms part of normal play.

Points can also be scored by forcing the offensive team to concede a 'Safety' score (worth 2 points). This is described in Chapter I.

There are several major distinctions between American Football and rugby, the first of which is associated with passing the ball. From every set-piece down, *one* forward pass is allowed (obviously by the offense) and it is worth noting that this pass must be delivered from the attacking team's side of the scrimmage line. In other words, a player in possession cannot hare off downfield and then throw a forward pass.

The second departure from rugby is that deliberate obstruction, known as 'Blocking', is quite legal. In doing this, a player is seeking to prevent the opposition from tackling the player of his own team who is carrying the ball. Again, the methods of blocking are strictly regulated and are to be distinguished from 'Tackling', which may be considered as using one's arms to encircle and hold an opponent. Significantly, a tackle, as in rugby, can be performed *only* on the player carrying the ball.

Free and unlimited substitution is allowed at all times of the game, between downs, to enable a player to perform his specialist role. In a 45-man squad there can be identified two groups of players, the defensive unit and the offensive unit, and in modern Football it is virtually unknown for a man to play both on offense and defense. One of the first things a new spectator notices, therefore, is the

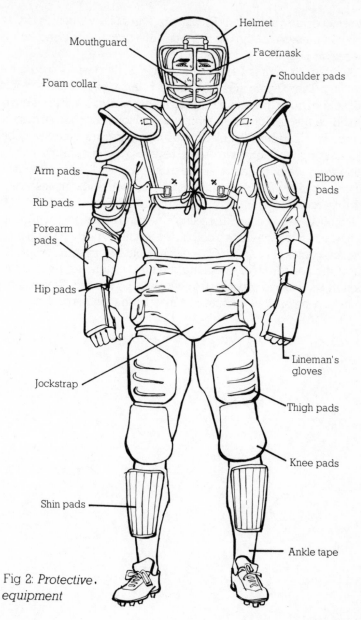

Helmet

Mouthguard

Facemask

Foam collar

Shoulder pads

Arm pads

Elbow pads

Rib pads

Forearm pads

Hip pads

Jockstrap

Lineman's gloves

Thigh pads

Knee pads

Shin pads

Ankle tape

Fig 2: *Protective equipment*

constant comings and going of players, particularly when, following a loss of possession, the offensive unit of a team is replaced by the defensive unit.

Another striking difference to rugby is the use of protective clothing. The players may look rather bizarre as they lumber onto the field, armour glistening in the sun. Yet even with this protection, which can weigh up to 25 lb, injuries which result in permanent disability still occur. The black and white photographs of the good old days, when men were men, reveal players sporting only a dog-eared leather scrum cap for protection. Sadly, in those days fatalities were not uncommon. Football was then, and remains today, a brutal game.

It is not to be expected that a single reading of this book will make a newcomer to American Football an instant expert on the game. The intricacies of no worthwhile game could be mastered so easily. But if the reader, after watching a game, returns to the book to identify some of the plays he has seen, then by the end of the season he should be as well informed as most of the long-term fans.

CHAPTER 1

SCORING POINTS

THE TOUCHDOWN DRIVE

By successfully gaining ten or more yards within each four-down series, the team on offense systematically moves the ball downfield until a touchdown is scored. A typical touchdown drive is illustrated by the following sequence of plays, beginning with the team in possession on its own 45-yard line, i.e. 55 yards away from the opposition goal line. Fig 3 shows this sequence diagrammatically.

1st down and 10 yards to go (described in commentaries as 1st and 10):

Play gains 4 yards and so the next down becomes 2nd down and 6 yards to go on the 49-yard line.

2nd down and 6 yards to go (2nd and 6):

Play gains 3 yards and so the next down becomes 3rd down and 3 yards to go on the opponents' 48-yard line.

3rd down and 3 yards to go (3rd and 3):

Play gains 7 yards and so the next down becomes 1st down and 10 yards to go because, by gaining 10 or more yards in three downs, another series of four downs has been earned.

1st and 10 on the 41-yard line:

Play gains 6 yards and so the next down becomes 2nd and 4 from the 35-yard line.

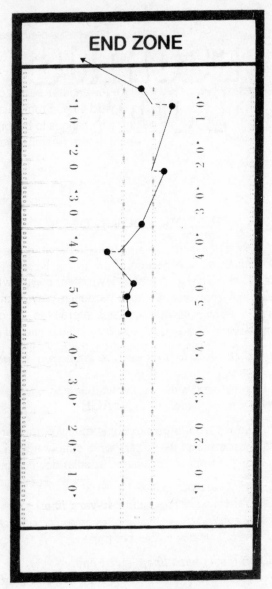

Fig 3: *The touchdown drive described in the text*

2nd and 4 on the 35-yard line:
Play gains 12 yards (more than the 4 yards necessary, hence earning another series of four downs).

1st and 10 on the 23-yard line:
Play gains 14 yards (more than enough for another series of four downs) and the ball is now on the 9-yard line. From this field position, the terminology for the next down changes to become 1st down and Goal to go (1st and Goal) because there remain fewer than 10 yards to go for a touchdown score.

1st and Goal from the 9-yard line:
Play gains 4 yards and so the next down becomes 2nd and Goal from the 5-yard line.

2nd and Goal from the 5-yard line:
Play goes into the end zone for a touchdown.

Note that in the diagram (Fig 3), each play (down) begins with the ball on or within the 'Hashmarks'. If a particular play terminates outside the hashmarks, the ball is moved laterally to the closest hashmark for the next down (indicated by a dotted line). If a play terminates at a point within the hashmarks, the next down begins with the ball 'spotted' at that point.

LOSS OF YARDAGE

As will become apparent later, the play from any particular down can result in a loss of yardage. This loss is simply added to the yardage which was required from that particular down to give the yardage needed for another series of four downs. For example:

1st down and 10 from the opposition 40-yard line:
Play *loses* 6 yards and so the next down becomes 2nd down and 16 yards to go, from the opposition 46-yard line.

2nd and 16 from the opposition 46-yard line:
Play *loses* 1 yard making the next down 3rd down and 17 from the 47-yard line.

SCORING A TOUCHDOWN

The formal requirements for the award of a touchdown, worth 6 points, are best exemplified by description of the two most common methods, namely 'Rushing' and 'Passing', by which the score is achieved.

Rushing Touchdown

The ball, which must be under the full control of the ball-carrier (the rusher) needs simply to break the vertical plane which extends directly upwards from the goal line. *The goal line is part of the end zone.* Unlike the requirement for a try in rugby, it is not necessary to

Fig 4. *The imaginary plane representing the front of the end zone*

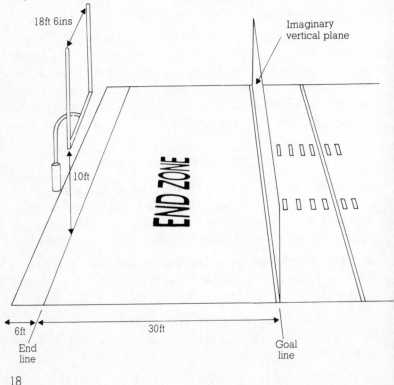

place the ball onto the playing surface. To this extent, the term 'touchdown' is misleading.

Passing Touchdown

An offensive player already in the end zone needs to catch and demonstrate his full control of the ball, which usually will have been thrown to him by the quarterback. If, as often happens, he has had to jump to catch the ball, he must land to touch the playing surface, with both feet within the end zone. It must be noted that *the side lines and the end (back) line are out of bounds* and therefore, his feet must not touch these lines in his initial contact with the playing surface. There is however, a supplementary rule which gives an advantage to the pass receiver who catches the ball (not necessarily in the end zone) in the process of being tackled. If, in the opinion of the referee, he would have landed in bounds but was driven out of bounds by the force of the tackle before his feet could touch the ground, the pass reception (touchdown if in the end zone) is allowed.

Obviously a player can score a touchdown by catching the ball within the field of play and running into the end zone, as described for a rushing touchdown.

EXTRA POINT ATTEMPT

Immediately following a touchdown, the offense kicks at goal from directly in front of the posts, the line of scrimmage being the 2-yard line. The kick, if successful, is worth 1 point and 'converts' the touchdown score of 6 to 7 points. A description of the extra point attempt is given in Chapter VII.

FIELD GOAL

On any one of the four downs, at any time, the offense can attempt a kick at goal, from a formal set-piece down. This, worth 3 points, is roughly equivalent to a penalty goal or drop goal in rugby, and will normally be attempted on 4th down, when within sensible range (up to about 40 yards) of the opposition goal line and in circumstances under which the gain of another series of four downs is unlikely (discussed later under PUNTING v FIELD GOAL ATTEMPT). If the kick, say from a down on the opposition 30-yard line, is unsuccessful, possession is transferred and the opposition initiates its counter-attack from that very same 30-yard line which was the original line of scrimmage. For an unsuccessful kick which was from within the opposition 20-yard line, play restarts on the 20-yard line. A description of the field goal attempt is given in Chapter VII.

CONCEDING A SAFETY SCORE

Occasionally, an offensive player will find himself in possession of the ball inside his own end zone. This can occur when the team on offense is deep within its own half. The unfortunate ball-carrier will have been obliged to retreat into the end zone in an attempt to evade the pursuit of defenders. If the defense can trap him inside the end zone, by establishing a firm hold or by tackling him to the ground, a safety score, worth 2 points, is conceded by the offense. Equally, if the ball-carrier can be forced to run over his own end line or side lines (all of which delineate the end zone), a 2-point safety is conceded. Once the ball-carrier is in the end zone, there is only one legitmate way out and that is in the forward (attacking) direction. To make matters worse, the team conceding the safety must restart play by kicking off from its own 20-yard line, which will always place the opposition in an excellent field position for an offense.

PUNTING

Punting is not a method of scoring but is most conveniently discussed in this section. On any one of the four downs, the attacking team can simply punt the ball as far as possible downfield. In doing this, possession is relinquished to the opposition who, on receiving the punted ball, will immediately attempt a return run which experience shows will be restricted on average to seven yards. The objective of the punt is to place the opposition deep in its own half from which position it will begin its formal return drive by the sequence of downs. However, it is a truism that in Football, as for every other game with the notable exception of grenade catching, possession is of vital importance. It is necessary to add, therefore, that to punt the precious possession away, which might appear an act of gross profligacy, is, on the contrary, a safety first and conservative strategy, as will be shown in the following section.

PUNTING v FIELD GOAL ATTEMPT

Let us imagine that the offense has used three downs in gaining 7 yards and yet is still on its own 30-yard line. From the fourth down play, 3 vital yards are necessary to earn another series of four downs and maintain the drive. Failure to gain these 3 yards on 4th down is disastrous, for handing over possession in the region of the 30-yard line is to place the opposition in a very dangerous field position from which to launch the counter-attack. Indeed, to risk transferring possession at any point within one's own half is considered nothing short of lunacy. Additionally, to attempt a field goal kick at goal posts which are barely visible in the unattainable distance, would be an act of equal madness. The conservative team, not willing to risk failure to gain the 3 yards, will, on 4th down, punt the ball away. The average net distance gained from a punt, after taking into account an average return run, is approximately 35 yards. In the case of a 30-yard line down, it follows that the opposition must start its counter-attack from, say, its own 35-yard line.

The situation is very different for the offense whose drive has come to a halt with just a 4th down left, but this time on the opposition 25-yard line. Again, to punt the ball away is an option but now there exists the possibility of a successful field goal attempt, failure at which would result in no significant positional disadvantage. Under normal circumstances, the offense would attempt the field goal for its reward of 3 points.

It should be mentioned that, for a team on offense yet losing by more than 3 points and with time running out, the kicking options are ignored. All four downs are used in the quest for that elusive touchdown. This results in exciting play, and the fans love it.

CHAPTER II

PLAYER POSITIONS

In the preceding chapter, methods by which the ball can be moved were given little consideration, so as not to obscure the overall view of the workings of the game. To anyone who has seen anything of Football it is trivial to say that these methods involve running with the ball, passing the ball or some combination of the two. A more detailed description of these can be absorbed only by first knowing player positions. The roles of each player in running and passing can then evolve.

THE SQUAD

The choreography of Football seems to require a cast of thousands. However, the reality is that a squad consists of forty-five players. Of these, some ten or so will take to the field only if both the specialist player and his replacement in a particular position are damaged beyond repair. Otherwise, this fortunate ten can view the carnage from the comfort of the squad bench, hence their 'title' of 'bench warmers'. Unlimited substitution is allowed at all times between plays, but at any one time a team will have only eleven players on the field. This will be the 'Offensive Unit', the 'Defensive Unit' or the 'Special Team'. Of these three, it is the special team whose role is least obvious. At this stage, it is necessary to say only that they will play in situations involving kicking, i.e. at the beginning of each half, for a field goal attempt, when punting or to restart after a score.

THE OFFENSIVE UNIT

The offensive unit in one of several standard formations is shown in Fig 5.

It is a legal requirement that there be *at least* seven players to form the 'Offensive Line', the limits of which are defined by the players at the extreme ends. In the example shown, these players are the 'Split End' and the 'Tight End'. Excluding these, the five grouped together, namely the 'Tackles', 'Guards' and 'Center', constitute the 'Interior Line'. Interior linemen are primarily guardians. They are the 'heavies' who protect the Quarterback or pave the way for the ball-carrier, who will almost always be a 'Running Back' or occasionally, the 'quarterback'. The split end and 'Flankerback' are primarily pass receivers. The quarterback directs the show by 'handing off' the ball to a running back or throwing a pass to a receiver. Of all eleven players, the tight end has to be perhaps the most versatile, playing on the one hand the role of interior lineman and on the other that of pass receiver.

So much then for the positions of the offensive unit and briefly considered responsibilities of the players who occupy them.

Fig 5: *Offensive unit: pro set formation*

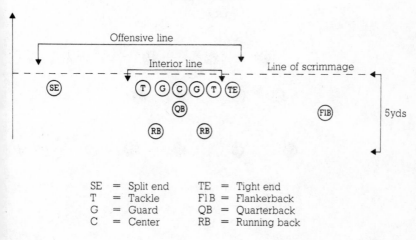

SE	= Split end	TE	= Tight end
T	= Tackle	F1B	= Flankerback
G	= Guard	QB	= Quarterback
C	= Center	RB	= Running back

THE DEFENSIVE UNIT

The defensive unit confronts the offensive unit and can also adopt many standard formations, one of which is shown in Fig 6.

The three defensive players, 'Ends' and 'Tackle', who line up face to face with the offensive line, constitute the 'Defensive Line' and will primarily attempt to ward off the aggressive intentions of the offensive line before tackling the ball-carrier. The four 'Defensive Backs' who are the 'Cornerbacks' and 'Safeties', have a responsibility to defend against the pass. The 'Linebackers', two outside and two inside, are required to identify the offensive play as either rushing or passing, before reacting to tackle the ball-carrier or assist the defensive backs in defending against the pass.

It is important to note that whereas movement of offensive players, immediately prior to the start of each play, is restricted (this is discussed later), players on defense are free to move around at will. Indeed, this they will do, particularly linebackers and safeties, in the attempt to create confusion for the offense. Typically, a safety and

Fig 6: *The defensive unit: 3-4-4 formation*

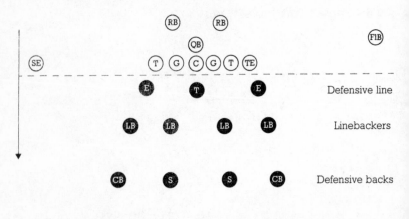

E = Defensive end   S = Safety
T = Defensive tackle   CB= Cornerback
LB = Linebacker

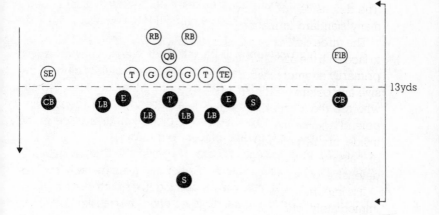

13yds

Fig 7: *Defensive unit immediately prior to the start of a down*

two cornerbacks might line up close to the line of scrimmage to await the start of play, before adjusting to defensive positions. Thus, the defensive unit may resemble the arrangement shown in Fig 7.

THE COMPOSITION OF A SQUAD

Almost without exception, every player in Professional Football will have spent four years in College Football. Far from being a market place free-for-all, entry into the professional ranks is rigidly controlled. All graduating college seniors are placed in a pool from which the professional clubs make selections in the order determined by their previous season's playing record. This is called the 'College Draft' and takes place in late April. The club with the worst record is given the first selection and the Super Bowl winners the last. Thus, in round one twenty-eight players are chosen. There are twelve rounds in all, selection in each one following the same order.

It may seem unfair on the best college player to be drafted by the worst club and it usually takes around a million dollars to ease the hurt. The arguments in favour of this system rest on the belief that, over a period of time, the playing strengths of each club will approach parity. Equally, the weakest club is virtually guaranteed a superstar from the draft, while no club with bottomless coffers can corner the market.

Not all college players will be selected. The unlucky ones who still wish to play professionally must travel from club to club, trying to impress coaches on the practice field. Many of those formally drafted will be quickly released to join these so-called 'Free Agents' doing the rounds. There is severe competition for a place in the allowed number of forty-five players per club.

Established players can of course be transferred, yet even here it is rare for cash to change hands. Rather, the arrangement involves the exchange of players, sometimes together with draft options. Thus a club entitled to a prime draft selection can transfer this option to another club, in exchange for an established player of high standing.

A 45-man squad will consist typically of the following:

Quarterbacks	3	Defensive linemen	7
Running backs	5	Linebackers	7
Wide receivers	4	Defensive backs	7
Tight ends	2	Kicker	1
Offensive linemen	8	Punter	1

NUMBERING OF PLAYERS

All players wear a shirt, numbered on the front, back and upper arm. This is not so much for the obvious reason, that of player identification, but more to indicate the *position* he will occupy and the role he will play. This is important in enforcement of the rules as each player, with some exceptions, is allowed to perform only certain acts. For example, interior offensive linemen are not allowed to receive a forward pass. The officials can easily spot a culprit by the number on his shirt. He may change his assignment to that of pass receiver, but only by informing the referee prior to the start of a particular play. The player positions (called 'Assignments') together with the range of numbers allowed, are as follow:

Quarterbacks, kickers and punters (all offense)	1–19
Running backs (offense), cornerbacks and safeties (defense)	20–49
Center (offense) and linebackers (defense)	50–59
Interior linemen (offense) and defensive linemen	60–79
Tight ends and wide receivers (split ends and flankerbacks)	80–89
Defensive linemen (in addition to 60–79)	90–99

CHAPTER III

OFFENSIVE PLAY

For anyone who has seen Football on television, however casually, some concept of an offensive play will have been gained. It will probably run as follows: 'One of the front linemen gives the ball to the quarterback who then retreats, before handing the ball to a runner, or throwing a pass.' This chapter will consider these basic processes and their subsequent developments.

The obvious place to start is with the quarterback, for he is the glittering star whose exploits, both on and off the field are most often discussed. Or should it be with the running back, who is probably the most highly paid and around whom, traditionally, a Football team is built? One could establish a case for the split end, whose blazing speed and magnificent hands will almost certainly have been featured in the pre-telecast promotion. Yet the reputations of these players can be built only on the foundation of a rock-like interior line, in the absence of which the offensive unit will be routed, so let us start with this.

THE INTERIOR LINE

The story, indeed the playing action, begins with the quarterback virtually straddling the center and barking out signals (these are understood only by members of his own team and are best considered as a countdown to the moment when the quarterback intends to begin the play). At a particular moment, pre-arranged in the

Fig 8:
*Center 'snapping'
ball to quarterback*

'huddle', the center 'snaps' the ball to the quarterback (see Fig 8) who, now at the controls, continues the play.

It is the choice of this play, either to run or to pass, which determines the responsibilities of the center in concert with his interior linemen. What is for certain is that, at all times, their job is to protect the ball-carrier whoever he may be. This they will do using nothing

29

Fig 9: *Illegal block from behind and below the waist, known as 'clipping'*

less than deliberate obstruction. Technically known as 'blocking', this is quite legal and can be performed to varying degrees by every player on the field. To consider the fine detail of blocking here would be distracting (it is discussed in Chapter X under Illegal Use of Hands, Arms Or Body). Briefly, an interior lineman may use the whole of his body above the knees in obstructing an opponent. However, he is *not* allowed to use his hands in an attempt to grab and hold. Additionally, for reasons of safety, any part of an opponent from the neck upwards, including his helmet and face mask, is forbidden territory. More heinous even than this is the illegal block from behind and below the waist, known as 'Clipping', and shown in Fig 9. This act of treachery invokes the maximum response, short of sending-off, by way of penalty.

Interior Linemen on Passing Plays

Immediately the ball is snapped, the interior line must make an initial and ferocious hit on the defensive line, which it is likely to outnumber. This is rapidly followed by a collective and gradual retreat to form a protective 'pocket', from which temporary sanctity the quarterback can await developments before delivering his pass. The protection pocket is shown in Fig 10.

Once in position, the interior lineman must hold his ground in the face of the onslaught from defensive linemen, linebackers and perhaps a safety. For a passing play of any magnitude, the quarterback needs a minimum of two seconds to allow for his pass receivers to run downfield, and clearly this 'pocket time' may be taken as a measure of the effectiveness of the interior line. A pocket time greater than three seconds brings with it enormous advantages, whilst anything less can spell disaster. In Super Bowl XV, the fortunes of the two teams could be traced back to the protection

Fig 10: *Quarterback in pass protection pocket. The split end, running back and flankerback have moved out to be in position to catch a pass*

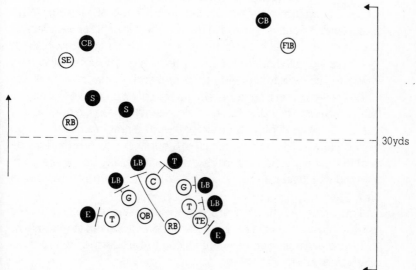

30yds

afforded to each quarterback. Jim Plunkett of Oakland was regularly allowed up to three seconds and won the award for being the game's 'Most Valuable Player', whereas for the defeated Philadelphia and a time-starved Ron Jaworski, it was a most miserable day.

An alternative strategy on passing plays might conceivably be for the interior line with its numerical superiority to obliterate the defensive line at the line of scrimmage. For two reasons, one legal and the other tactical, this does not happen. Firstly, on a play resulting in a forward pass, the interior linemen are not allowed to travel more than one yard beyond the line of scrimmage until *after* the ball leaves the passer's hand. It follows that the forward momentum gathered by the interior lineman, and delivered in the initial collision, must be controlled so as not to infringe this law. Secondly, a defense alerted to expect a pass play will reinforce its defensive line with linebackers and perhaps a safety, taking closer order. Defensive players, then in superior numbers, would almost certainly find their way around the ends of the offensive protective line. The formation of a pocket is the natural adjustment to counteract this.

Interior Linemen On Rushing Plays

On receiving the snapped ball, the quarterback takes two or three steps away from the line and 'hands off' the ball to a runner. Back at the line of scrimmage, the clatter of helmets to a background strain of grunts signals that the battle to create a gap is under way. It is towards this turbulence and mayhem that the ball-carrier rushes.

In one sense, on passing plays the role of an offensive lineman is the passive one of wait-and-see before reacting. On the other hand, his part in rushing plays is an altogether different business – he can now go to war. He must dominate his opponent. This he will do by hitting the man in an upward direction and raising him to the point beyond which he is betrayed by his own centre of gravity, as shown in Fig 11.

This achieved, the forward drive, generated by enormous leg power, must be maintained and the opponent shoved to this side or that, to create the gap through which the ball-carrier will rush, as illustrated in Fig 12.

Fig 11: *Offensive lineman (No 54) blocks defensive player (No 60)*

Success depends not merely on strength, for this will be matched, but rather on its application with perfect timing and at the correct angle of rise. The offensive lineman has the advantage in timing since he knows the precise moment at which the ball will be snapped. However, if his upward angle of thrust is not correct his momentum will be misdirected (too high or too low) and the contest, being inconclusive at best, will represent a loss to the offense. For out of stalemate at the line of scrimmage, the defense emerges the winner since the offense has been restricted to little or no gain in yardage.

As an alternative to the frontal assault, the play may be designed to run around the end of the offensive line. In this case, an interior lineman assumes the role of travelling guardian. Closely following

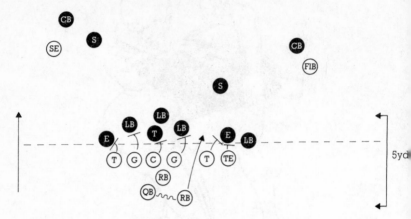

Fig 12: *Creation of a gap in defensive line: blocking by right guard and right tackle. The running back aims for the gap between right guard and right tackle*

the snap and rather than confronting his opposite number, the guard will pull away from the line to sweep around the end, leading the ball-carrier into open field. Now on the rampage and towing his running back, he needs to execute a clean block on the approaching defender, usually a linebacker or safety, thus releasing the ball-carrier for further gain. For a play directed to the right side, either the right or left guard might pull away from the line to lead the rush, as shown in Figs 13 and 14.

There is little doubt that much of the success achieved by the great running back is attributable to the blocking protection of his offensive guard. Running behind Reggie McKenzie, O.J. Simpson of Buffalo became a legend in the early seventies. For the remainder of the decade, the story was that of Pittsburgh's Franco Harris breaking all Super Bowl records, behind the blocking of Sam Davis. The same is no less true in the eighties; indeed, even the most ardent Tony Dorsett fan would acknowledge the contribution made by Herb Scott, the high speed Dallas battering ram.

It is a natural sequence then, that following the consideration of the role of the offensive lineman should be that of the running back.

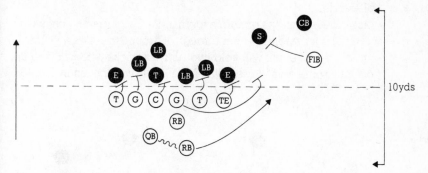

Fig 13: *Right guard leads rush down right side*

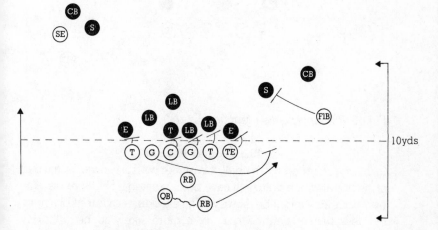

Fig 14: *Left guard leads rush down right side*

THE RUNNING BACK

From its beginning, Football was traditionally a running (rushing) game. However, the successive rule changes of the seventies have shifted the balance in favour of the passing offense. The running back still plays an important part for he too is a legal pass receiver. This aspect of his game is discussed more appropriately under the heading of PASS RECEIVERS; this section will deal with his role as ball-carrier.

In simple terms, the quarterback 'hands off' to a running back who will try to gain yardage either through or around the offensive line. A normal offensive unit will field two running backs who will take up positions some four yards behind the offensive line, as in Fig 15.

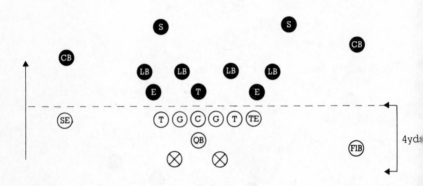

Fig 15: *Running backs identified by* ⊗

The Frontal Assault

In theory, on receipt of the ball, the runner will rush towards that part of the line at which a gap will have been created by his linemen. The playing reality might be, however, an altogether different business. Far less than a definite gap, it is more likely to be a barely discernable chink of daylight, a seam. It is through this that the runner must penetrate. Furthermore this seam might well material-ize in an unexpected part of the line. In his four-yard build-up the runner must therefore be reading the effectiveness of his interior linemen before exploiting the opportunities gained by their efforts. With maximum force, head down and shoulder pointing, he hits the seam and takes whatever yardage he can, together with the inevitable beating. From the resulting pile-up the officials will decide, one way or another, that he has gained one, perhaps two yards. So it's 2nd and 8 yards to go with thirty seconds on the clock (see Chapter IX) before the next play must begin. He stoops in the collective huddle, head still ringing, to hear the quarterback call the next play: 'Okay guys, same again.'

Of course it isn't always like this for he can reasonably expect that, say once in four times, a reasonable gap will be there, but even so there will still be opposition. Having cleared the line of scrimmage, he will be confronted by a linebacker. However there is now some help available; the other running back has not been standing idly by. When the gap opens his responsibility is to lead the ball-carrier much as would an offensive guard. A clean block on the linebacker by this lead blocker will spring the ball-carrier into open field where he can now wreak havoc. A fifteen-yard gain is possible and, against a defense which has erred in placing its safety wide and at the line of scrimmage, a fifty-yard touchdown run is not uncommon. This block by the second running back is shown in Fig 16.

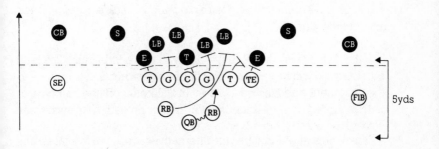

Fig 16: Running back blocks for ball-carrier

Such then are the fluctuating tasks and fortunes of a running back in making a frontal assault. Should he choose the attack around the end of the line, a similar situation exists.

Around The End (The Sweep Play)

After an initial one-yard move in a forward direction, the ball-carrier in an around-the-end play will veer off to one side, hoping to exploit an open field weakness. The initial forward move is made in an effort to influence linebackers to hold position behind their offensive line, which would be normal in defense against a frontal attack. If the linebackers are fooled, the chances of success are increased dramatically. Again, a great deal depends on the outside blocking protection the ball-carrier will receive, now from perhaps both a guard and tackle together with the other running back, shown in Fig 17.

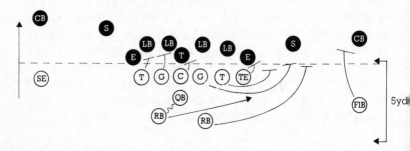

Fig 17: *A run around the end with blocking by tackle, running back and pulling guard*

If the defense is not fooled the play will make little gain. The lead blocking trio will be swamped by linebackers crossing to cover and the two safeties advancing to assist. In all likelihood, the ball-carrier will be forced over the side line for little or no gain. The successful cover is shown in Fig 18.

It may be self-evident that the alternative tactics of a frontal assault and an end run require of the running back different physical qualities. Indeed, the most effective pairs are those in which one has power and durability and the other brilliant speed and agility. Such a combination was that of Larry Csonka and Eugene 'Mercury' Morris, in the early seventies. With Csonka going up the middle and Morris around the end, Miami dominated the NFL for two seasons

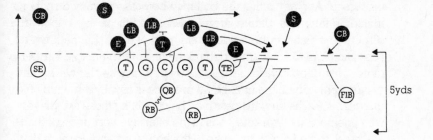

Fig 18: *Linebackers, safety and cornerback cover an end run*

and well into a third. Such combinations are, however, rare, and a team will normally possess just one outstanding running back. In the whole of the NFL, some sixteen or so players will gain somewhere between 1000 and 1700 yards in a sixteen-game season, at an average of 4.5 yards per attempt. The real workhorses, such as Earl Campbell of Houston and George Rogers of New Orleans, will carry the ball twenty-five times in a game, and in this bruising occupation it is not surprising that most running backs undergo major knee surgery. In support of the star, there will be two or three other players, some still learning and others past their best, who will grind out 300 yards, at an average of 3 yards per attempt, when not required to block for the star man. At this end of the spectrum, Football is less than glamorous. Still, the breakaway run for a touch-down is a spectacular sight and happens with such searing pace that one is advised not to blink. Curtis Dickey of Baltimore has a fastest time of 10.15 seconds for 100 metres, and before my athletics friends make reference to those wind-assisted, downhill, hand-timed races in Loonyville, USA, let me hasten to add that in his final College year, he beat every major American sprinter on the track. Down in Dallas, they reckon that Tony Dorsett is even faster.

PASS RECEIVERS

One major departure from rugby in the rules of American Football, namely the legality of deliberate obstruction, has previously been discussed. Another is that the ball may be passed in any direction, including forwards. Unlike lateral passes and those in a backward direction, which can be made at any part of the field, the forward pass can be made only from behind the line of scrimmage. Furthermore, only one forward pass is allowed. It can be thrown by any player from behind the line, but in practice is usually thrown by the quarterback. The forward pass may be caught by those two players who line up at the extreme ends of the offensive line, and additionally by all those who, at the snap of the ball, are standing more than one yard back from the line of scrimmage. These so-called 'eligible receivers' are shown in Fig 19.

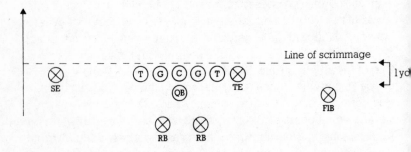

Fig 19: *Eligible receivers marked by* ⊗

If the ball is not caught, the play is ruled as an 'incomplete pass'. The game clock is stopped and play resumes at the original line of scrimmage but with the loss of that particular down. For example, say on 2nd down and 10 from the 45-yard line, a forward pass is not caught (incomplete). The next play becomes 3rd down and 10 from that very same 45-yard line.

Passing plays are conveniently described under three headings: short, medium and long.

Short Pass

The short pass is used in circumstances when only two or three yards are required to gain another first down. It is usually directed towards the side line and only rarely over the middle. As a valuable alternative to the running play, especially with defensive players massed in the middle area, it gives width to an offense and allows the receiver to read the distribution of the defense before threading his way downfield. For the short pass, a running back is usually the intended receiver. Fig 20 shows the positional play.

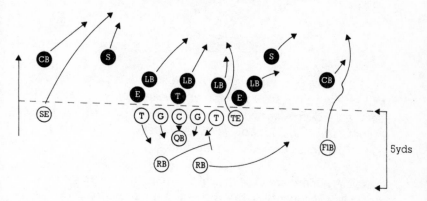

Fig 20: Running back takes up position for short pass. The tackles, guards and center form a temporary pocket, together with one running back. Split end, tight end and flankerback make decoy runs, with defensive backs and linebackers almost certainly dropping back to cover

To use a running back in this way has been a significant and noticeable tactical development of the past two seasons and it is not uncommon for him to make four receptions in a game, gaining, on average, eight yards per catch. As always for a sizeable gain, lead blockers are indispensible. These will be the other running back, the tight end and the guard pulling away from the line of scrimmage, shown in Fig 21 overleaf.

The Medium Pass

With the medium pass, we come to the specialist pass receivers who take up wide positions on or behind the line of scrimmage.

41

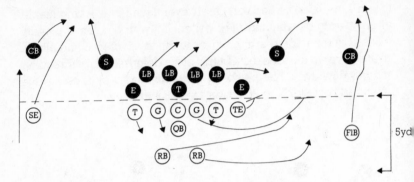

Fig 21: *Blocking for running back receiving short pass. The guard, tackles and center form a temporary pocket. Split end and flanker-back make decoy runs with some defensive players dropping back to cover. Running back adopts a lateral position to make the reception, allowing blockers to take up stations*

Classically, there are two types of pass, one down the side line, the other over the middle. The medium pass down the side line is simplicity in itself. In execution, the intended receiver runs down the side line, stops, turns his back to the defending cornerback and makes the reception. By turning, he effectively shields the ball, thus guarding against an interception by the defender. This manoeuvre is shown in Fig 22.

For the play to succeed, the stop and turn must be in rapid sequence and after instant and yet heavily disguised deceleration by the runner, previously travelling at maximum speed. A gentle slowing down would reveal the play to the marking cornerback who will not need a second hint. Having made the reception, the receiver will attempt to make forward progress, almost certainly by cutting infield and, alas for him, into the welcoming arms of the safety. It is perhaps the weakness of the side-line pass that the receiver is hemmed in by this very side line. On the other hand the side line can represent salvation for both him and his team. Firstly, by stepping out of bounds he will avoid the savage tackle from the cornerback whose area has been violated. Additionally, for a team

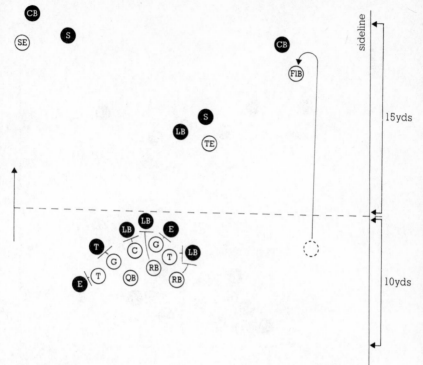

Fig 22: *Medium pass down the sideline: the hook pattern. The quarterback drops back in the pass pocket. Split end and tight end run decoy patterns*

losing and with time running out, by stepping over the side line he can stop the game clock.

For a defensive alignment which has its linebackers tightly in support of the defensive line and its safeties lying back to defend against the long pass, there is a no-man's land. It is this that the medium range pass over the middle is designed to exploit, as shown in Fig 23.

The pass trajectory will need to be such as to clear the line of scrimmage and inevitably the ball will be caught by the receiver leaping high into the air, as Fig 24 shows. Having been watching the

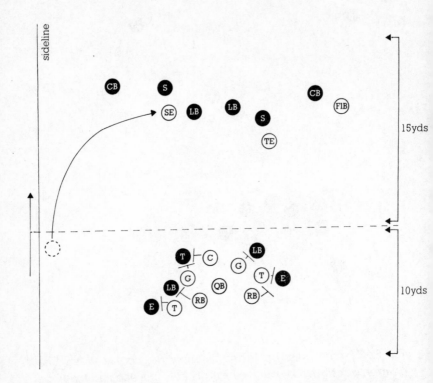

Fig 23: *Medium pass over the middle. The quarterback is in the pass pocket. Tight end and flankerback run decoy patterns. Two linebackers and defensive backs, recognising a pass play, have dropped back to cover*

evolving pass play and by now recovering to defend, the safety will deliver a crushing tackle on the receiver who, with both feet off the ground, exposes himself to the risk of severe injury, particularly to his back. It is a feat of great skill in catching and an act of extreme courage for the receiver who, by retaining control of the ball until grounded, completes the reception. This thorax of a defense is no place for the faint-hearted.

44

Fig 24: *Wide receiver catches pass in heavy traffic*

The Long Pass

This most difficult pass to execute, the long pass is spectacular and dramatic, and is the killer strike. On completion, a pass receiver with even the least sense of occasion, will stride majestically into the end zone, ball triumphantly held aloft in acknowledgement of the pandemonium from the stands. The so-called 'bomb' pass will be delivered to coincide with the arrival of the receiver who will have

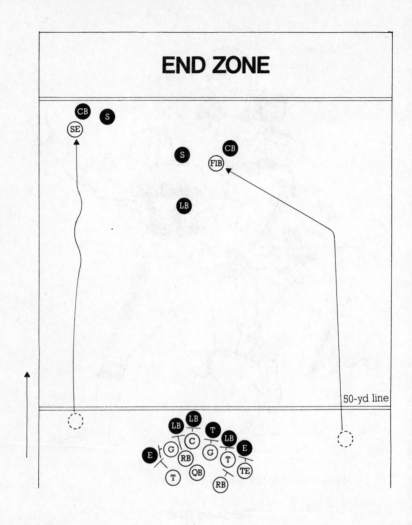

Fig 25: *Long pass to deep middle or corner. The quarterback is in the pass pocket. Split end runs the flag pattern (i.e. towards the corner). Flankerback runs the post pattern (i.e. towards the posts)*

run either close to the corner or over the middle and deep, as shown in Fig 25.

The route taken by the pass receiver, not always direct, is known as his pass pattern. This he will run for the greater part, not looking for the ball until the last few feet of its flight. To turn his head prematurely would alert the defender who could well be in close contact and keeping pace.

In a section devoted to offensive play such as this, the opportunities open to a defense have been omitted for clarity and reserved for later. But with both wide receiver and cornerback homing in on the ball, it would be quite wrong to defer discussion of the defensive option. Simply, once the ball is in the air it belongs to whoever can catch it. It is a major achievement if the defense can intercept the pass, for not only will a touchdown have been prevented but they can immediately counter-attack. However, in attempting to catch the ball, any illegal contact which would take the form of bumping and holding, by either player, is severely penalised. Pass interference by the offense nullifies any gain which may otherwise have been made (discussed in the Rules section). For a guilty defense, the penalty is the award of an automatic 1st down to the offense, with play restarting at the point of infringement.

The wide receivers (split end and flankerback) will almost certainly possess searing pace; indeed a track time for 100 metres of greater than 10.5 seconds is considered slow. Both the fabled Bob Hayes of Dallas and, more recently, Johnny 'Lam' Jones of New York Jets, are former Olympic sprint champions (Jones won a Gold in the sprint relay race). Indeed, the NFL is littered with merchants of high speed, for example, James Lofton (Packers) and Wesley Walker (Jets). Yet speed itself is not enough, for to it must be added the ability to catch the ball, under both the attention of defenders and the pressures of the occasion. There are however, a select few players who graced the game and yet may be described as being 'slower than the fastest', and of these the former Oakland Raider, Fred Biletnikoff, springs to mind. Using subtle change of direction, superb catching skills and more than a little guile, Fred left the game as the fourth best leading receiver of all time.

THE TIGHT END

With the possible exception of quarterback, there is no playing position in football which demands more in the way of physical presence and technical skills than the position of tight end. In consecutive plays, he may have to block like an offensive tackle, lead like a guard, take a medium pass in the congested middle area or sprint to the end zone to receive a bomb. The standard dimensions of a tight end are six feet four inches tall and closer to seventeen than sixteen stones in weight.

As a blocking lineman, his job on running plays is to anchor the offensive line and in particular, for running plays around the end, to 'turn in', thus blocking off an avenue of pursuit, as shown in Fig 26.

Fig 26: *Tight end blocking on running plays around the end*

As a blocker on passing plays, he is a key element in the evolving pass protection pocket. His assignment will be to control the defensive end, shown in Fig 27.

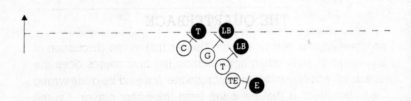

Fig 27: *Tight end in the pass protection pocket*

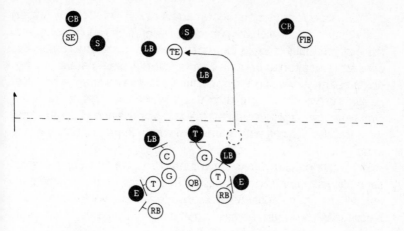

Fig 28: *Tight end runs for pass over the middle. Split end and flankerback act as decoys*

As a pass receiver, he is in no way restricted to a particular pass pattern but his height clearly makes him the most suitable target for the medium pass over the middle and into the teeth of trouble. This is shown in Fig 28, and is not unlike drawing the short straw.

It is a feature of the modern game that this aspect of the tight end's play, pass receiving, assumes even greater importance than ever before. Men such as Kellen Winslow (San Diego), Ozzie Newsome (Cleveland) and Dan Ross (Cincinnati) have responded to the call, and they pose a severe threat as passing targets, certainly equivalent to that of the wide receivers.

THE QUARTERBACK

It may be of some surprise to the reader that in the discussion of offensive plays, only when approaching the final stages does the quarterback appear under the microscope. It would be quite wrong for it to be inferred that he is the least important player. On the contrary, nothing would succeed without his skills. In those things which we have considered, he is at the nerve centre.

The prime requirement of a quarterback is intelligence. Other individual players will have particular assignments and to complete them successfully is to do their jobs. Yet the quarterback must be constantly monitoring the collective result of these separate components before exploiting the opportunities by releasing the ball. He needs the vision of both depth and width in order to take in, simultaneously, these complex interactions. Having done this, he must transfer the ball with a timing in which there is no margin for error.

His active playing duties conveniently resolve into four areas: to hand off to a running back, to pass to a receiver, to run with the ball himself and, in the absence of a sensible alternative, to 'scramble'. Before these however, he has to go through the starting count drill leading up to the snap of the ball.

The Starting Count Drill

Before each down, the offensive unit goes into a collective huddle to allow the quarterback to explain the next play. The players then take up positions and the quarterback, now straddling the center, begins the formal starting count. A full count would sound something like the following:

'Red 36, Red 36, Set, Hut(1), Hut(2), Hut(3).'

The colour.number code, Red 36, is to confirm to his own players that the prearranged play is still on. Following the 'Set', offensive linemen must remain motionless. To coincide with one of the 'Hut' signals, one, two or three, the specific 'Hut' being known only by the offensive unit, the center snaps the ball and all hell breaks loose.

Occasionally, once at the line of scrimmage and having read the disposition of defensive players, the quarterback may feel that the chosen play will not succeed. He will alter the play, *at the line of scrimmage*, by changing the colour-number code. The count would then become:

'Red 36, Red 36, Blue 22, Blue 22, Set, Hut(1), Hut(2), Hut(3).'

The whole of the offensive unit will of course be aware that 'Blue 22' signals a late change and equally, the new play to which 'Blue 22' refers.

Running Plays (Rushing Plays)

The quarterback's part in rushing plays is perhaps the most simple of his duties. He needs merely to hand the ball to a running back. Yet even here, his movements leading up to the hand-off can be of great assistance to the runner. By rolling to one side or the other (play action) and by pretending to hand off to one runner before handing to the other (faking), he can momentarily mislead the linebackers, who can react to defend only when the offensive play has been read with certainty. The hand-off itself must be with tender loving care since a fumbled ball can be recovered by anyone, including the defense, from the ensuing shambles. With the hand-off successfully completed, he will make a discreet withdrawal. He is allowed to block opponents, but for a player of his strategic importance and relatively flimsy padding, it would be to take a needless risk of injury.

Passing Plays

It is on passing plays that the quarterback earns his bonus, and for these the quality of his throwing arm must be beyond question. He will throw a twenty-yard pass with little or no arc in flight, or alternatively hit a target fifty yards away and moving. On each play, there will be both a primary and a secondary receiver, the latter becoming the target only if the former is effectively covered. Should both players be inaccessible, the quarterback will look for another eligible receiver, usually a running back, who will have taken up a position of little strategic importance and yet free from defensive cover. This running back, known as the 'safety-valve', will function simply to allow the quarterback to get rid of the ball, as shown in Fig 29 overleaf.

Bootlegging

There are occasions when the quarterback will assume the role of ball-carrier in that, rather than handing the ball to a specialist running back, he will hare off into an open space. This is known as 'bootlegging'. He will attempt to gain rushing yardage but always in anticipation of the impending tackle, before which he will voluntar-

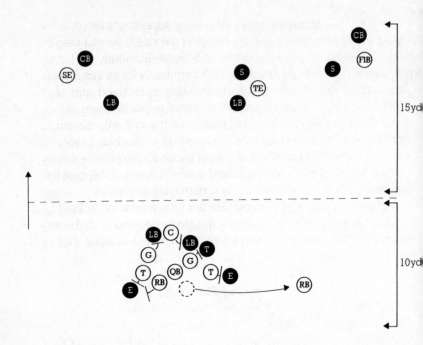

Fig 29: *Running back acts as safety valve. The quarterback is in the pass pocket but all downfield receivers are marked*

ily go to ground or hop over the side line. It is valuable as a surprise tactic, and typically a quarterback will average six yards on two or three attempts per game. However, as with blocking, rushing is a bruising business which carries with it the high risk of injury. The thoroughbred quarterback is far too valuable to make a habit of it.

Scrambling

By courtesy of his offensive linemen, the quarterback will operate from a pocket, and with luck, this will remain intact for up to three seconds. However, even the most secure pocket will eventually collapse, and with defenders pouring through gaping holes, this pocket, designed for his protection, becomes the place of his entrapment. For the quarterback with nowhere to run and all receivers marked, all is not yet lost. Using what might be called a 'professional alternative' (i.e. by bending the rules) he can pass in the direction of a legal receiver and yet deliberately under or overthrow to enable the ball to bounce harmlessly for an incomplete pass. As described previously, possession is retained and play restarts from the original line of scrimmage on the next down. However, should the referee adjudge that the ball was thrown to ground, with no receivers within five yards of the ball, purely to avoid being tackled for a loss of yards ('sacked'), the offense will be penalised by a loss of ten yards *and* a loss of down. If the quarter-back in danger of being sacked disregards this devious ploy, he can run for his life – he can 'scramble'. He does not want to be tackled for a loss of yards; indeed he does not want to be tackled at all. He will therefore scramble around in a most undignified manner, before hopefully escaping to safety over the side line.

CHAPTER IV

DEFENSIVE PLAY

Earlier in this book the defensive players were briefly introduced. The diagram (Fig 6) illustrating their playing positions was purposely exaggerated to establish clearly that a defense consists of three elements: linemen, linebackers and defensive backs. Though it is a simplification, this model will be retained for its value in supporting the descriptions of players' responsibilities. It is worth repeating that, immediately prior to the snap, linebackers and safeties may well adopt positions close to the defensive line. Yet it remains true that, regardless of the initial positions they adopt, their defensive responsibilities are essentially unchanged.

DEFENSE AGAINST A RUNNING PLAY

The Frontal Assault

The offensive linemen will be attempting to establish a gap for the running back. As will become apparent from subsequent sections, it is often possible for a defense to anticipate with confidence the type of offensive play it will face. On other occasions though, it will be a matter of allowing the offense to initiate a play before reacting to defend. This is particularly true for linebackers and defensive backs. The defensive lineman on the other hand, knows for certain that he will be in collision with offensive linemen on every play, whether it be run or pass. The instant play begins, the defensive lineman will therefore need to absorb this initial contact and very rapidly read the play as run or pass. On a running play, the subject of this section, the offensive lineman is *not* restricted in his downfield movement, and his commitment to a forward and unqualified surge will quickly be detected by the defensive lineman as signalling this running play. His first tasks are not to lose ground, to fight against being shifted to one side or the other, and to prevent the creation of a gap. Should these objectives be achieved and the offensive surge controlled, there is the opportunity for counter-attack by penetrating the offensive line, now in some disarray, to tackle the ball-carrier, not yet at the line of scrimmage, for a loss of yards.

It is a most unlikely event for the defensive linemen alone, outnumbered as they are, to achieve such a success, but of course they are never alone. Immediately the play has been identified as a rush, the linebackers will spring into action, plugging a gap should it appear, or penetrating a weak spot in the offensive line to tackle the ball-carrier. There will even be extra assistance from safeties for they too, having identified the play as a rush, will rapidly advance, as shown in Fig 30.

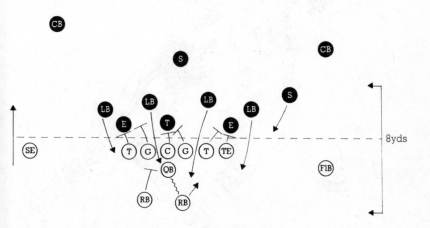

Fig 30: *Linebackers and safeties defend against the rush*

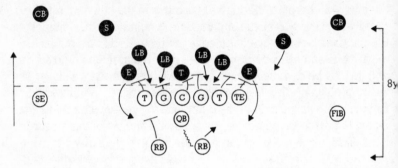

Fig 31: *Defensive ends charge running backs from around end of line*

The physical requirements of a defensive lineman are obvious. Dismissing all talk of size and weight, the defensive tackle is best described as an enormous brute. The defensive end is all of this and

Fig 32: *Defensive end tackles quarterback*

usually equipped with respectable speed, since for him there is always the possibility of charging the running back or quarterback from around the end of the line, as shown in Fig 31, with the desired result shown in Fig 32.

The linebacker is the hunter killer who, never taking his eyes off the ball-carrier, will attack with reckless abandon. Fig 33 shows a linebacker alert and ready for action.

Fig 33: *The linebacker in 'ready' position*

Defensive backs are always fast and must be able to execute a clean open field tackle, since theirs will be the responsibility to bring down not a faltering, barging runner in a melee but rather the man freed from his shackles and approaching maximum speed.

So much then for defending against the frontal assault. For a running attack around the end, the attempted penetration will focus some five yards or more to one side, along the line of scrimmage. For the defense, the emphasis changes to become one of speed of reaction and pursuit.

The End Run

The defense must react to confront an offense attempting to shift the point of attack away from the congested middle and hoping to profit from surprise. Indeed, with this advantage, the early indications always are that the offense will succeed. Yet to set up a blocking pattern using pulling offensive linemen and perhaps a flankerback, and to reach the advantage line (scrimmage line), takes time. In the early stages of the attack, defensive linemen will be left temporarily isolated at the scrimmage, and delayed on the near side by the tight end. Linebackers however, will detect the play and begin the cross-field move to defend, as shown in Fig 34.

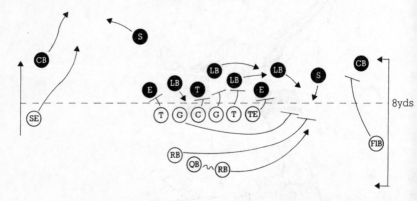

Fig 34: *Linebackers and safeties react to an end run. Left guard pulls to right side to lead the runner. Split end runs decoy pattern*

58

There are occasions when the alert linebacker, anticipating or sensing the play before its commencement, will direct colleagues to the point of attack. With good reaction timing, a wall of linebackers reinforced perhaps by two safeties, will force the ball-carrier laterally and ultimately out of bounds, as shown in Fig 35.

If the cross-field cover is established more quickly even than this, the ball-carrier will be forced to seek a route by turning inside and into the clutches of defensive linemen arriving belatedly on the scene. An end run, if successful, is a magnificent expression of collective offensive power, but should it fail, it is a lingering death for the running back.

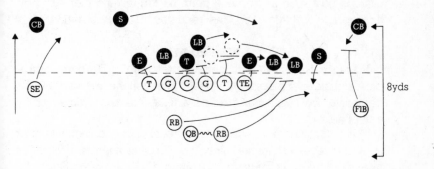

Fig 35: *Linebackers and safety have anticipated end run*

DEFENSE AGAINST A PASSING PLAY

For a short pass in the middle area, the responsibility for defending falls to the linebackers, but for all other passes the defensive backs go to work. These are the four players, two safeties and two corner-backs, who are out and out pass defenders and on whom this discussion is primarily centred.

There are two major philosophies of pass defense. The first of these involves the close marking of all pass receivers, 'Man For Man'; the second is to guard open spaces, the 'Zone Defense'. The

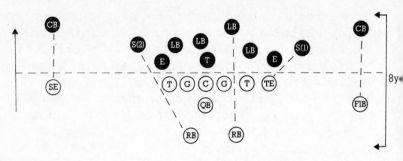

Fig 36: *Man for man marking. The opposing players are linked by dotted lines*

latter is best seen as evolving from the former and therefore it is appropriate that 'Man For Man' receives first consideration.

Man for Man

In the normal offensive formation, illustrated in Fig 36, there are five potential pass receivers. Of these, four will be marked by the defensive backs with the fifth and least likely receiver picked up by a linebacker.

The defensive backs will try to establish close contact with their assigned receivers immediately the offensive linemen drop back from the line of scrimmage, signalling a passing play. Safety (1) closely marks the tight end whilst safety (2) will take up close order with the advancing running back. For the safeties then, it is a question of waiting before acting. On the other hand, the corner-backs, who are marking wide receivers, have the option to play 'bump and run', described as follows. Within five yards of the line of scrimmage, the cornerbacks are allowed to make one blocking contact with the receivers, opposite whom they line up. When play begins and *before the ball is in the air*, the cornerback can block the receiver to the ground, the object being to delay the receiver at the line of scrimmage. This initial block is, however, a risky business for if the cornerback should stumble, the receiver who can avoid the block will escape into open field, unmarked and leaving the cornerback stranded at the line of scrimmage. More often the cornerback, discarding the risk, will seek to establish and maintain body contact, constantly adjusting position, and by this gentler and more subtle art of obstruction, delay the receiver.

There reaches a stage however, when this jostling moves out of the five-yard area and the quarterback is winding up for the pass. It now becomes a chase. The receiver will hare off on his down field pass pattern with the cornerback in close contact and running stride for stride. With both players homing in on the ball, decision time for the cornerback is fast approaching.

His prime responsibility is to prevent the pass completion, and this he will do by knocking the ball to the ground (he will bat the ball away). The pass is incomplete, the ball is ruled dead and play will restart with the next down, back at the original line of scrimmage. This is the no nonsense, safety first, procedure. Alternatively, at all times the cornerback can attempt to intercept the pass and this he might do by stepping or jumping in front of the receiver, at the last possible moment. Fig 37 shows a defensive back competing for the ball. This though carries the risk that he may deflect the ball, which can still be caught by the receiver. He may even miss the ball completely and disastrously. Nevertheless, on average, a cornerback will make five interceptions in a season and there is always the possibility of the moment of triumph, the glorious interception return for a touchdown.

There remains a third choice, which is used when the wide receiver has manufactured space for himself and is clearly going to catch the ball, with the cornerback in no position either to knock the ball away or to intercept. In this case, the cornerback's only option is to deliver one almighty tackle on the receiver at the precise moment he makes contact with the ball, in the hope of preventing a complete reception. In this last resort, the timing of the tackle must be perfect. If the tackle is too early, this and any other form of contact will be ruled as pass interference. If too late, it will succeed only in preventing further gain after the completion.

It is reasonable to assert that man-for-man marking carries an element of risk, in that the defensive back must have lightning reflexes, and a running speed equal to that of the receiver. It was

Fig 37: *Defensive back competes for ball with wide receiver*

from recognition of this that the more conservative 'Zone Defense' evolved.

Zone Defense

Before a detailed consideration of the zone defense is made, it is appropriate to consider once more what happens at the snap of the

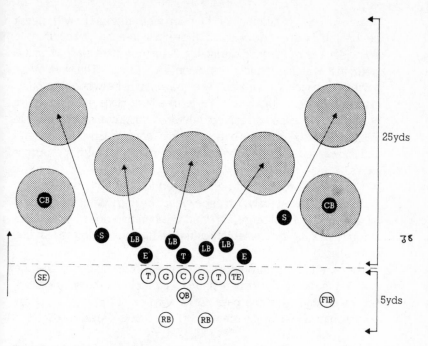

Fig 38: *Establishing a zone defense. This is only one of several zone systems that are used*

ball. Five receivers could well scatter into the defensive backfield. Of these five, one will be a primary target, a second will be on standby and the remainder will act as decoys. To defend against this multiple pass offense, the defensive backs and two or three linebackers are allocated areas of authority called zones, shown in Fig 38. The defensive player is responsible for the receiver who enters his zone. The moment the receiver leaves, he becomes the responsibility of someone else. The picture then is one of a distribution of defensive players, holding station amidst the complex pattern running of offensive receivers. Once the pass is on its way, the target is immediately obvious and at this stage, all defenders converge to the point of reception.

The theory of the zone defense lies in the belief that defenders, declining the challenge of man-for-man marking, will never be beaten badly. Additionally, there will be the opportunity to engage in closer marking during the flight time of the ball, when it is clear just which receiver has been picked out. The weakness, however, lies in the vulnerability of the junction between two zones, since a receiver in this position is as free from close marking as it is possible to be. If the ball can be delivered quickly and accurately to this junction, the chances of a successful completion are high, and with slowly reacting defenders, the opportunity for further progress exists.

The modern squad will be equipped to play both man-for-man and zone defense, and will change tactics during a game depending on circumstances of scoreline, field position and down status. Consideration of the factors which influence that choice forms part of a later chapter.

There remains a third approach to pass defense, namely the one seeking to defeat the play at source, by tackling the quarterback before he can send the pass on its way, or at the very least, by putting him under great pressure. This is considered next.

The Pass Rush

Consideration of the approaches to pass defense thus far have been made on the assumption that the quarterback will have all the time he needs to deliver the perfect pass. There are occasions in Football when the pass can be predicted with certainty, for example when the offense is losing the game, time is running out, the end zone is far in the distance and it is 3rd down and several yards to go (this would represent a rather miserable situation for the offensive team). In this case, the defense would saturate its territory with pass defenders, willingly giving up rushing yardage and virtually ignoring any attempt to attack the quarterback. However, when a pass is expected and the defense can sense a quarterback's diminishing composure, a defense bristling with confidence will rush the wretched man. This will require the use of a body of defensive players in numbers, greater than can possibly be contained by offensive linemen. Known as 'Blitzing Play', this is not without its

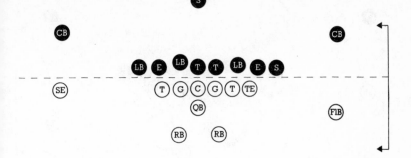

Fig 39: *Defense in readiness for the blitz. Note that there are now four defensive linemen, two ends and two tackles*

risks, for to assemble defenders at the line in readiness for the cavalry charge is to leave the rear sparsely populated and vulnerable should the quarterback do the unthinkable by getting the pass away. A formation in readiness for the blitz, might look something like that in Fig 39.

The list of impositions enforced by a defense with such numerical superiority is impressive. The formation of a pass protection pocket is out of the question. The quarterback, almost certainly under pressure from penetrating defenders, will be forced to shift position, and though he is not yet reduced to scrambling, the possibility of a successful long pass becomes remote. As the pressure of the blitz increases and with distant receivers now obscured by bodies, large and looming larger, the scramble begins and down goes the quarterback.

However, for an offense which correctly anticipates a blitz, there is a way out. To an offensive ball-carrier protected by a blocker or two, a thinly populated rear defense represents easy pickings. Of course, the trick is to release this ball-carrier from the line of scrimmage. The offense, expecting the blitz, will go to the line of scrimmage, never intending to contest the physical battle, and disdaining to stem the rush. At the snap of the ball, two offensive linemen, a guard and tackle, will immediately withdraw to re-

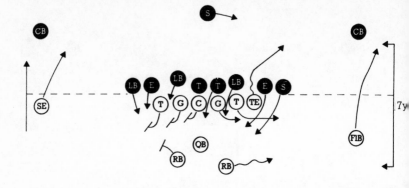

Fig 40: *Early stage in the screen pass play. The quarterback drops back into passing position. Right guard and right tackle withdraw to right after partial block. Tight end slips past defensive end after partial block. Running back discreetly filters off to right. Split end and flankerback run decoy patterns*

establish position on one side of the field, roughly parallel to the scrimmage line. A running back too will descreetly filter out to this same side. The hope is that to the blitzing throng, blinded by the hunger for quarterback meat, this shift will go undetected. The quarterback needs only to loop the ball over the head of the blitzing defenders, to the wide running back who, with the screen of two blockers, will now go to town. This so-called 'Screen Pass' is the simple and effective counter to the heavy pass rush. Figs 40 and 41 show how the screen pass is executed.

The Personalities

Throughout the first forty years of the NFL, offensive players held the stage while those on defense, whose job was to stifle, spoil and prevent, went largely without public acclaim. Quite properly, the last twenty years have seen some correction of this imbalance. As individuals and in groups, defensive players now pose for the posters.

David 'The Deacon' Jones, defensive end of the Rams, had no

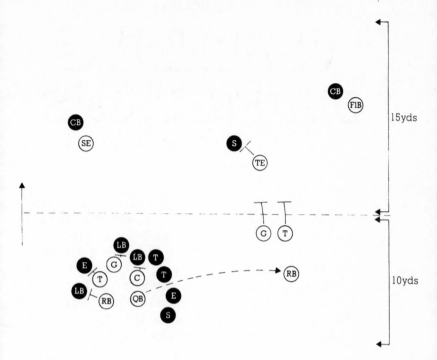

Fig 41: *Execution of the screen pass*

peer. Dallas had its 'Doomsday Defense' and Minnesota, 'The Purple Gang'. Denver went to Super Bowl XII on the strength of its 'Orange Crush' and Pittsburgh dominated the late seventies with 'The Steel Curtain'. The story continues into the eighties with the Jets, who appear to have the makings of a wrecking crew in the shape of 'The New York Sack Exchange', whilst Miami has its 'Killer Bees'.

Linebackers too are not to be kept out of the picture as the 'Crunch Bunch' of New York Giants would attest – and who would dare argue?

Defensive backs haven't yet joined in the name game, but Lester Hayes (Raiders), Kenny Easley (Seattle), Nolan Cromwell (Rams) and Ronnie Lott (San Francisco) present a fearsome sight.

CHAPTER V

OFFENSIVE FORMATIONS

So far, the actions of offensive players have been considered on the basis that the offensive team takes up the same standard formation immediately prior to the snap of the ball. To the television viewer, there must appear to be a bewildering variety of formations and, focussing on the quarterback as he does, the cameraman does not make it easy to follow what is going on elsewhere. In reality, a team will use one of a small group of formations. These, together with discussions of their strengths and weaknesses, appear below. The following notation is used in the Figures:

Q = Quarterback	**FB** = Fullback
RB = Running Back	**TB** = Tailback
SE = Split End	**HB** = Halfback
FlB = Flankerback	**WB** = Wingback
TE = Tight End	**C** = Center
T = Tackle	**G** = Ground

The Standard Pro Set

From the pro set (Fig 42), all standard plays are possible and they can be directed to either side. The advantage is that it does not reveal the play to the defense. The flankerback stands back from the line of scrimmage, enabling him to be a legal pass receiver. Were he to be on and functioning as the end of the offensive line, the tight end would no longer be eligible to receive a pass. A drawback is that in allowing for itself all the options, there is little opportunity to provide extra weight in support of a particular play. In subsequent formations, provision for the reinforcement of the rush or pass is made.

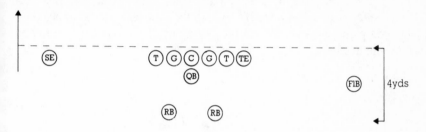

Fig 42: *The pro set formation*

The I Formation

In the I formation (Fig 43), the center, quarterback and two running backs stand directly in line with each other. One running back becomes the fullback, the other the tailback. This formation is a slight variation from the pro set and, while still not betraying the intention, gives the tailback an advantage. The fullback is in a better position to act as lead blocker and some tailbacks feel that there is a fraction more time to assess the possibilities at the line of scrimmage.

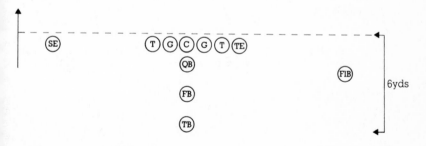

Fig 43: *The I formation*

The Power I Formation

As its name implies, the power I formation (Fig 44) is a reinforcement of the I formation, effected by the introduction of another running back (now called a halfback) at the expense of a flankerback. From this, a running play is indicated with now both the halfback and fullback able to lead the ball-carrying tailback. With only one receiver wide, the possibility of a long pass is virtually eliminated.

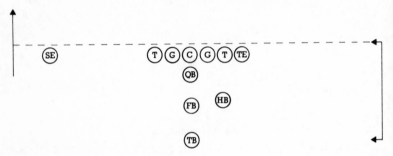

Fig 44: *The power I formation*

The I Slot

From the I slot formation (Fig 45), the ball-carrying tailback has two lead blockers but this time at the expense of the tight end position. Blocking on the line of scrimmage is of course weakened. In compensation, there can be two wide receivers on the line, since validation of the now absent tight end as a pass receiver is no longer a consideration.

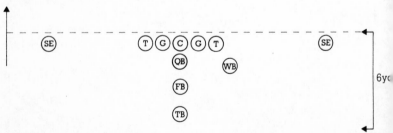

Fig 45: *The I slot formation*

The T Formation

The T formation (Fig 46) is clearly designed for a running play. The quarterback can select from three running backs and has a full complement of blockers at the line of scrimmage. With only one wide receiver though, the opportunities for a pass are poor.

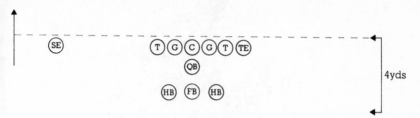

Fig 46: *The T formation*

Short Yardage Formation

In the short yardage formation (Fig 47), the offense is totally committed to the run. It is used therefore only when short yardage is required, either for a touchdown or to gain another first down. The ball-carrier will often leap over the pile of linemen rendered prostrate by the mayhem at the line, as is shown in Fig 48 overleaf.

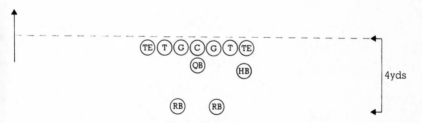

Fig 47: *The short yardage formation*

The Twin Set

The twin set, also known as the slot formation (Fig 49), concentrates two pure pass receivers on one side at the expense of neither line blocking nor a running threat. It may well appear to be easing the

71

Fig 48: *The running back (No 31) takes the air route*

problems of pass defense and yet, by running their pass patterns in mutual sympathy, the two receivers can cause the opposite effect.

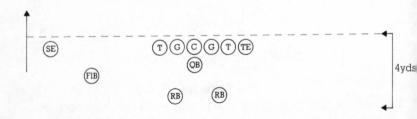

Fig 49: *The twin set (also known as slot formation)*

The Spread Set

The spread set (Fig 50) is clearly a passing formation with potentially five receivers. The two running backs will stand up at the line of scrimmage and yet far enough away to retain their eligibility as pass receivers.

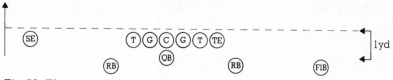

Fig 50: *The spread set*

The Shotgun Formation

The shotgun formation (Fig 51) is identical with the spread set, except in the position of the quarterback and of the tight end, who moves wider. By standing some five yards back from the line of scrimmage, the quarterback has greater time to read the disposition of defensive players. A disadvantage is that the longer snap required from the center weakens his effectiveness as a line blocker. From this formation, a running play is most unlikely.

The shotgun had been out of favour for twenty-five years before, in the late seventies, it was successfully revived by the Dallas Cowboys. More recently, this lead has been followed by Buffalo and Philadelphia.

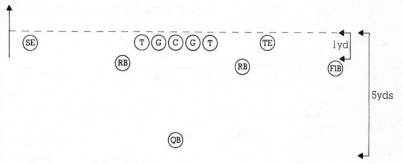

Fig 51: *The shotgun formation*

Interchange Of Formations

It may be part of the offensive strategy to set up the scrimmage using one formation, before changing to another, prior to the snap of the ball. The intention here is to disguise the type and direction of the play. The change may be subtle, for example in the transformation of the I formation to the pro set, as shown in Fig 52.

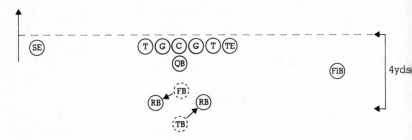

Fig 52: *Interchange of formation from I formation to pro set*

Alternatively, the adjustment may be of greater magnitude and strategically more significant as in the transformation of the pro set to the twin set, shown in Fig 53.

For this, whilst the quarterback is calling signals at the line of scrimmage, the flankerback will run laterally 'in motion' to take up his new position. He must not however make a move in the offensive direction before the ball is snapped, for this will be penalised and

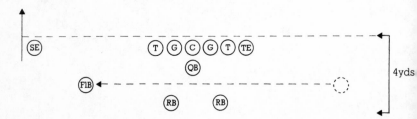

Fig 53: *Interchange of formation from pro set to twin set*

any apparent gain resulting from the play will be nullified. The run of the flankerback is one of the easiest moves for the new 'television fan' to spot.

CHAPTER VI

DEFENSIVE FORMATIONS

Playing good defense is largely a matter of anticipating what the offense will do. This is not always guesswork. In particular, in the final quarter of the game, the combination of scoreline, field position and time remaining will virtually dictate the course of action likely to be chosen by the offense. It is possible to identify several defensive alignments, which for reasons of clarity are illustrated showing players essentially in three lines. However, movement in defense, prior to the snap of the ball, is not restricted as it is for offensive players. Defensive linemen will shift from side to side and linebackers will repeatedly charge forward and withdraw. Cornerbacks may line up nose to nose with wide receivers, and safeties may stand just off the shoulder of the defensive end.

Each of the following formations is best regarded, then, as showing starting positions, for each of which subtle adjustments are made. In the Figures for these formations, the following notations are used:

E   = Defensive End
T   = Defensive Tackle
LB = Linebacker
CB = Cornerback
S   = Safety

4-3-4

The 4-3-4 formation (Fig 54) is one of the two commonly used when it is not possible to anticipate the offensive play. A four-man front will generate an effective pass rush. Three linebackers are sufficient to reinforce the defensive line facing a frontal assault, to provide lateral coverage against the end run and to defend against the short pass over the middle. Four defensive backs are adequate for pass coverage.

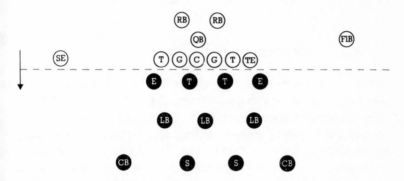

Fig 54: *4-3-4 formation*

3-4-4

The 3-4-4 formation (Fig 55) is the other formation commonly adopted. Indeed in recent years there has been a marked increase in its popularity. It is felt that the extra linebacker gives greater effectiveness against the frontal assault, but it is slightly vulnerable against a pass since the weaker pass rush, by only three linemen, allows the quarterback a longer time to select his target.

Pass Defense Formations

When the offense needs a gain of greater than seven yards on a particular down (usually 3rd down) to maintain the momentum of its

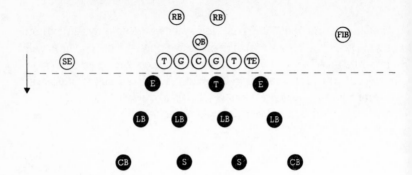

Fig 55: *3–4–4 formation*

drive, a pass may be safely anticipated. Defensive backs are therefore reinforced at the expense of linebackers. The following formations can be seen as evolving from the 4–3–4 and are varying shades of so-called 'Prevent Defenses'. The moment play begins, linebackers and safeties will usually set up a patchwork of zones, since this is considered the most effective way of preventing the long pass completion. Cornerbacks may initially play man-for-man, before withdrawing to join the zone system. The following three formations retain the capability to mount a pass rush.

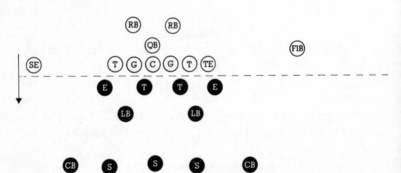

Fig 56: *4–2–5 formation, also known as the nickel defense*

4–2–5, the Nickel Defense

In the nickel defense (Fig 56), the defensive backs are reinforced by a safety, at the expense of a linebacker, affording *five* pass defenders. Thus the term 'nickel', which arises through allusion to the coin which has a 5-cent value.

4–1–6, the Dime Defense

In the dime defense (Fig 57), two linebackers are replaced by safeties, and the name 'dime' arises by allusion with the coin of increased value.

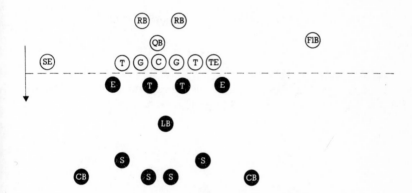

Fig 57: *4–1–6 formation, also known as the dime defense*

3–1–7, the Penny Defense

I have not the remotest idea why such an insignificant coin as the penny should be victimised in description of this most bizarre of formations (Fig 58). Indeed, it should not go unmentioned that the penny defense, an innovation of the eighties, is designed for use only in the most hair-raising of circumstances.

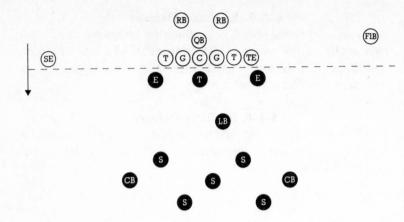

Fig 58: *3–1–7 formation, also known as the penny defense*

5–1–5

As an alternative philosophy, to combine a heavy pass rush with a well-stocked backfield, but again at the expense of linebackers, the defense can choose a 5–1–5 formation (Fig 59).

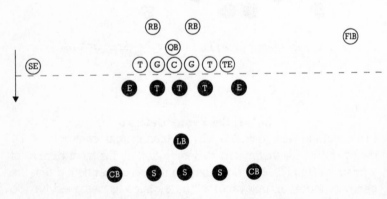

Fig 59: *5–1–5 formation*

7–1–3

In defense of what may be inches of ground, say close to the end zone, where the offense will use a short yardage play, a seven-man front line will be used. A frontal offensive assault is most likely, but to counter the surprise pass, three defensive backs are retained in the 7–1–3 formation (Fig 60). Needless to say, all potential receivers will be closely marked, once the ball is snapped.

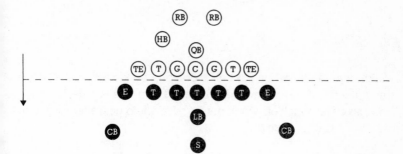

Fig 60: *7–1–3 formation*

CHAPTER VII

SPECIAL TEAMS

In circumstances when the ball is going to be kicked, both offense and defense will bring on their 'Special Teams'. There are four such occasions: at a kick off, when punting, for a field goal attempt and in converting a touchdown.

THE KICK OFF

The team which wins the toss has a choice of two options: (a) to kick off or receive the kick, or (b) to select which goal to defend. At the beginning of the second half, the team which lost the initial toss now has the choice. It is therefore possible, though unlikely, that a team will kick off at the beginning of each half. More usually, a team will opt for facing the kick-off, with its opportunity to start a drive with a four-down series. In addition, to restart the game after a touchdown, with or without successful conversion, and after a successful field goal, the scoring team kicks off. This is another difference with rugby, in which the team which has just scored receives (faces) the kick off. Figures 61 and 62 show the likely positions of the players at the kick off.

In the formal circumstances described above, a team kicks the ball, supported by a plastic tee, from its own 35-yard line, and it is immediately of great importance to consider the regulations governing possession. At any point following the kick off, the receiving team can gather the ball and establish possession. However,

Fig 61: *Kicking team in readiness for the kick off*

once the ball has travelled 10 yards, or has been touched by a player of the receiving team, the kicking team can gather the ball and gain possession. Not wanting to present the opposition with good field position which would result from a short kick, the kicking team will thump the ball as far as possible downfield. From this, one of three things can happen.

Firstly, if the ball passes through the end zone (unlikely), the opposition restarts play with a four-down series from its own 20-yard line. Secondly, if an opposition player establishes possession, within his own end zone, but declines any run back, again play restarts at the 20-yard line. Finally, from any point of the field, including the end zone, the opposition player might run the ball back up the field

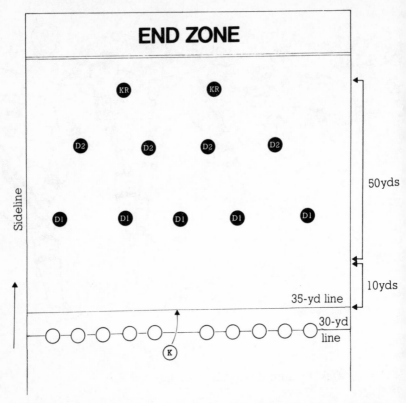

Fig 62: *Player positions for a kick off. The defensive players marked D1 are in readiness for short kick off (unlikely) before dropping back to form blocking pattern together with defensive players marked D2. Either of the kick return specialists marked KR will catch the ball, with the other blocking on the return run*

until he is grounded. Play then restarts with a four-down series on or inside the hashmarks, corresponding to the point at which the runback was halted.

It is important to re-emphasise that at all times during the kick off play, the kicking team will compete for possession. Thus, if the kick receiver fails to gather the ball, the kicking team can recover possession. Furthermore if, during the kick return, the ball is fumbled (dropped) either accidentally or as the result of a tackle, it can be recovered by the kicking team, which then becomes the team in possession and on offense.

In normal play, the kick return specialist will catch the ball some five yards out from his own end zone, and will immediately begin the return run. Taking care to remain behind the ball until it has been kicked, all eleven players of the kicking team will tear downfield to tackle the runner who, as always in Football, is not alone. His own team will be blocking the opposition, not in a haphazard way but in a collective effort to establish and maintain a corridor, along which he can run freely. In extreme cases, he will go 'all the way' for a touchdown, as did Fulton Walker of Miami in Super Bowl XVII. More usually the return run will cover some 25 yards.

For the kicking team, the emphasis will be on downfield pursuit, and the squad will therefore contain several speedy linebackers and defensive backs. The kick return squad, for which the emphasis will be on blocking protection, will consist largely (literally) of offensive linemen. The requirements of a kick returner must closely approach those of a running back but, as it is a tough job, the star runner will never be risked. The responsibility usually falls to the first or second year player, still learning his trade and playing second or third fiddle to the established running back pair.

Finally, as a point of law, if the kick off goes out of bounds (over the side line) without having been touched by a player of either team, the kick is retaken, but now from the 30-yard line of the kicking team. In effect, the kicking team suffers a 5-yard penalty.

PUNTING

There is a world of difference between a kick off and a punt. Firstly, punting takes place from a down position (a set piece scrimmage), usually on 4th down. Secondly, the specialist punter will have to catch the ball tossed directly backwards (long snap) by the center, before applying the boot. In addition, the opposition will charge the punter in an attempt either to tackle him, or at the very least deflect

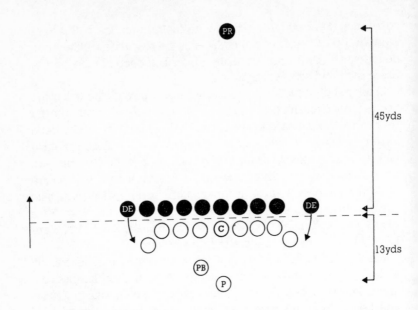

Fig 63: *Player positions for the punt. The punt return specialist, marked PR, awaits the punt. The defensive ends, marked DE, will charge the punter. The punt specialist blocker, marked PB, waits to protect the punter if necessary. The punter, marked P, awaits long snap from center, marked C*

the ball. A punt is therefore very different from a kick off which takes place in unhurried circumstances and from a specific field position (35–yard line).

Another difference is that the punting team can send two wide players downfield, *at the moment the ball is snapped.* This means that, even before the ball is punted, there will be two potential tacklers already some ten yards closer to the specialist punt returner than would be the case from a kick off. To amplify this advantage, the punter will hoist the ball as high as possible, giving maximum 'hang time'. Once on its way then, the punt is not unlike the Garyowen or 'up an' under' of rugby. Player positions for the punt are shown in Fig 63 and the punter in action in Fig 64.

Fig 64: *The punter in action, protected by two blockers*

The unfortunate punt returner is in the position of waiting to catch the ball, falling from on high, to the ominous thunder of approaching footsteps. One of three things usually happens. By raising his arm, he can signal his intention to make a 'fair catch'. If he can complete the catch, he must not be tackled, but at the same time he is not allowed a return run. Play restarts with a 1st down at the point of the fair catch. As a second option, he can ignore the ball, allowing it to land, bounce and roll harmlessly downfield. He is safe in this since, *if he does not touch the ball*, then neither can the punting team. Play restarts with a 1st down at the point where the ball comes to rest. If this point is in the end zone, play restarts from the 20-yard line. Finally, he can catch the ball and attempt a return run, with the usual blocking support, though now less effective than for a kick return. Again, should he fumble, possession can be re-established by the punting team which then regains offensive status. It is not surprising that a punt return will go for an average of seven yards only.

As a point of law, should the punted ball go over the side line, play restarts with a 1st down to the receiving team, from the hashmark corresponding to the yardage marker of the point where the ball went out of play. To take advantage of this, the punter will attempt to kick the ball out of play as close as is possible to the opposition goal line, since this would pre-empt any return run. Clearly, this point would be close to the cornerflag, in the region known as 'Coffin Corner.'

FIELD GOAL ATTEMPT

For a field goal attempt, which is equivalent to a penalty goal or drop goal in rugby, there are three key players: the center, the holder and the kicker, whose positions are shown in Fig 65. The center tosses the ball backwards (long snap) to the holder, in a kneeling position, who places the ball on the ground for the immediate kick.

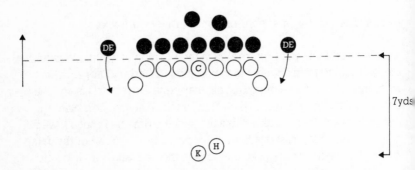

Fig 65: *Player postitions for a field goal attempt. The holder, marked H, awaits a long snap from the center, marked C, to place the ball for the kicker, marked K. The defensive ends, marked DE, will charge the kicker around the ends*

Fig 66: *The holder (No 85) holds the ball for the kicker (No 10)*

This is shown in Fig 66. All kicks take place from a set piece scrimmage position. The distance of the kick can be misleading, because the actual kick takes place from a point some seven yards back from the scrimmage line, and the goal posts are based on the back line of the end zone. Thus a kick originating from a down on the 25-yard line will have to travel 42 yards to clear the crossbar. Should the kick be unsuccessful, play will restart with a 1st down to the opposition on that very same 25-yard line which was the original line of scrimmage.

The defending team will attempt to charge the kicker from around the ends of the line, and also to block the kick with a well-timed leap. The kicker must therefore achieve early elevation of the ball. This presents a problem for the longer, say 50-yard, kick since, for this, the greater carry requires an initially lower trajectory.

'FAKE' FIELD GOALS AND PUNTS

It should be remembered that, even after setting up to take a punt or field goal attempt, the kicking team may choose to try to gain a first down by running or passing the ball, since after all it is still a 4th down play. Of course, a kicking formation is hardly conducive to rushing or passing success, and yet the element of surprise is in favour of the kicking team. On a 'fake' field goal play, the holder will pretend to place the ball down for the kicker before rolling out, either to run with the ball or pass to a receiver who will have drifted downfield, as surreptitiously as possible. To allow for this possibility, the holder is often a reserve quarterback.

On a 'fake' punt play, the punter makes no bones about it. On receiving the snapped ball, he will run for daylight (and his life) always with the knowledge of just how many yards are needed to gain a 1st down and maintain the momentum of the drive.

The success of 'fake' field goals and punts depends upon surprise, an element which is lost if the tactic is overdone, so not many will be seen in a season.

TOUCHDOWN CONVERSION

For a touchdown conversion, or extra point attempt, the line of scrimmage is the 2-yard line, and again the crucial feature is the smooth transfer of the ball from the center, via the holder, to the kicker. This achieved, the kick of approximately twenty yards from dead centre is simple. A specialist will miss one or two whilst kicking forty in a sixteen-game season. There is however no margin for error, since a bad snap from the center or a fumble by the holder, gives the kicker no time for recovery. Figure 67 shows the player positions for a touchdown conversion.

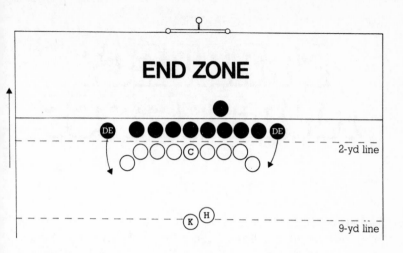

Fig 67: *Player formation for a touchdown conversion. The holder, marked H, awaits a long snap from the center, marked C, to place the ball for the kicker, marked K. The defensive ends, marked DE, will charge the kicker around the ends*

CHAPTER VIII

STRATEGY AND TACTICS

Team strategy is the prerogative of the Head Coach, and whilst he may well delegate matters of tactical detail to his assistant coaches, he is the general with overall control. He will almost always instruct the quarterback on what the next play should be. He will do this either by using a coded hand signal from the side line or, exploiting the free substitution rule, he will send on the information with the replacement player.

He will be indeed a fortunate coach if his team is powerful both in rushing and passing. More often, an offense will be based on the strength of its running backs and, of the seventy or so down plays, forty will be rushing plays. This would be a conservative tactic, though not without the possibility of a big gain, and it is a relatively simple matter to gain two yards on each play, perhaps even three. However, taking account of the odd mistimed hand-off or misdirected play, this would be insufficient for maintaining a long drive. Invariably, to keep risk to a minimum, the coach will opt for a mixture of the rush and the short pass to either side of the field. An offense which is able to move the ball consistently and which starts to put together 1st downs, is said to establish 'momentum'. With this comes the confidence to attempt more ambitious and sophisticated plays, though they carry a greater risk of failure. These, for example the long pass, can bring instant success in the form of a dramatic touchdown.

One may well wonder why there is virtually no lateral passing in

American Football, since to string together a series of passes, as in rugby, is quite legal. However, should the ball go astray during transfer from one offensive player to another, bouncing erratically as it would, it could be recovered by players of either team. Curiously, and I am not aware of the philosophical basis for the rule, should the defense recover the ball, it may *not* be advanced as part of that play. This is to be contrasted with the recovery of a fumbled ball, that is, a ball dropped by a player previously in full control, which *may* be advanced. To this extent, turning over the ball to the opposition during a lateral passing sequence is not quite the catastrophe a fumble would be. Nevertheless, running the risk of relinquishing possession is considered, in itself, sufficient reason to restrict lateral passing only to the most desperate occasions.

For the defense, which is of course aware of the strengths of the opposition, there is always a problem. They may well try to guess the intentions of the offense and against, say, a suspected powerful rush, reinforce the line by all four linebackers taking close order and with a safety up at the line of scrimmage. Yet to do this weakens the defensive backfield and will serve to enhance what may otherwise be a moderate passing threat. On the other hand, a defense can pay closer attention to potential pass receivers, but only at the expense of numbers at the line of scrimmage, thus enhancing the rushing potential of the offense. Under normal circumstances, early in the game and when prediction of the imminent play is impossible, a standard 3–4–4 formation will be adopted. In this, the two central linebackers will be concerned primarily with the frontal assault whilst the two outside linebackers will play with pass defense in mind.

As has been said before, several factors, alone or in combination, can sometimes virtually dictate the type of play to the offense. These involve the down status, field position, scoreline and time remaining on the game clock.

On 3rd down and with six or more yards to go for another 1st down, a pass is most likely. On the other hand, as the offense moves closer to the end zone, and the defensive backfield becomes increasingly congested with players, thus increasing the risk of interception, and particularly when only short yardage is required for a 1st down, a running play is more than likely.

For a team losing by three or fewer points, the offense may well settle for manoeuvring into field goal position, discarding the more ambitious objective of a touchdown. Here, a safe rushing play or short pass is usually preferred.

When the offense is losing by a margin greater than three points, and is some way from the end zone with time running out, a passing play is a certainty. This, though, need not necessarily be a bomb, since the long pass against a defense primed to expect it has a poor chance of success. The wily quarterback will often opt for the short or medium pass down the side line. Once completed, the receiver can step out of bounds, in this way stopping the clock. The whole play may take up only five seconds of game time and by this means, the offense can leapfrog down the field in less than a minute. This is the so-called 'Two Minute Drill', since it is the last resort, usually reserved for the final two minutes of the half.

CHAPTER IX

PENALTIES, TIMING AND THE OFFICIALS

PENALTIES

Penalties are assessed in terms of yardage lost by the offending team. A minor infringement will cost five yards whilst those involving moderate physical contact or significant technical violations cost ten yards. For an act of horror, usually associated with the possibility of serious injury, fifteen yards are charged. In the extreme case of unqualified violence, the player is sent off. The referee does not pussyfoot around; the rules are rigidly enforced and the players do not usually complain. However, unlike the case in most sports, only the individual offender is penalized; he may be replaced legally by another player.

The system is best explained from the starting point of a simple example, with the offensive team at 1st and 10 on its own 30-yard line. Play begins and the result is a 12-yard pass completion, but during this, an official spots an infringement by the *offense*. He does *not* blow a whistle, he does *not* stop play from continuing, but rather he throws down a yellow flag at the point of infringement. The play is allowed to run its full course until the ball is dead and signalled as such by a whistle. The referee then has a discussion with, in this case, the defending team captain, who is given the option to accept or decline the penalty ruling. Obviously, he will accept and the offensive gain will be nullified. If the judgement is a 5-yard penalty, the ball is returned to the original line of scrimmage, and then taken a further 5 yards back. The team on offense retains possession and is now on its own 25-yard line, but more importantly, *it retains the former down.* Play resumes with a 1st and 15, on the 25-yard line.

There will be occasions when it would be to the disadvantage of the defending team to accept the penalty judgement. For example, let us assume again the offense on its 30-yard line, but now at 4th and 10. Suppose the play was a 7-yard gain, but in the process the offense incurred a 5-yard penalty. If the defending team accepts the judgement, the ball is placed on the 25-yard line and play resumes with a 4th and 15. Yet by accepting the apparent benefit of a 5-yard penalty against the offense, the defense is allowing the offense to replay that 4th down. They are being allowed another opportunity to gain a 1st down, another bite at the cherry. Sensibly, the defending team captain would *decline* the penalty for, since the play had gained only 7 yards, the team on offense would have to transfer possession to the team on defense, in accordance with the four-down/ten-yard system.

The same holds true for the team on offense, in the event that the defending team commits a foul. For example at 4th down and 7 yards to go, on its 30-yard line, the offense gains 9 yards on the play, during which the defense is guilty of a foul incurring a 5-yard penalty. Were the offense to accept the judgement, the 9-yard gain would be nullified and they would be required to replay the 4th down which would then be 4th and 2 yards to go, from the 35-yard line. The 5-yard penalty would be *declined* since, by having gained 9 yards on the play and ignoring the penalty allowance, the offense has earned another series of four downs.

In certain cases, a loss of down is automatic following infringement by the offense, particularly in circumstances associated with passing the ball (discussed in the Rules section). Additionally, for a guilty defense, a yardage penalty might be added on to the gain made by the offense resulting from that play. For example, if during a successful pass play, a defender 'roughs' the passer (discussed in Rules section), the 15-yard penalty would be added to the yards gained by the successful pass.

The application of advantage preceded by discussion, is not

unique to American Football. In rugby, there is choice following infringement at a line-out (throw-in not straight), and for offside after a punt. In soccer too, advantages may be applied, but in this the referee is sole arbiter, and there is no discussion.

TIMING

The game is played in four 15-minute quarters, with a 15-minute break (half time) between the second and third quarters. However, a whole game, including half time, will last in excess of three hours, because when the ball is not in play, the game clock is stopped. This leads to a great deal of stopping and starting, which can initially be an irritation for British fans accustomed to the continuous play of soccer and rugby. Yet it makes sense for two good reasons. Firstly, the fans pay to see an hour of Football, this in itself being sufficient reason for regulating the duration of play. Secondly, it prevents the sordid exhibition of time wasting, which is seen in many games, particularly soccer. So it is of no use to belt the ball into the stands, to feign injury, or to hold onto the ball whilst taking up position after having conceded a free kick.

Generally the game clock will run whilst normal play is in progress and the ball remains inbounds. For all those occurrences which would lead to the loss of valuable playing time, the game clock is stopped.

There are two clocks in operation. One is the game clock which indicates the time remaining in the quarter. The other, the 30-second clock, is used only to regulate the time between downs. It is perhaps best to illustrate the workings of the timing system by describing a drive downfield (normal play).

From the moment the ball is positioned onto the playing surface by the official, the 30-second clock starts. This allows the quarterback 30 seconds to initiate play by taking the snap from center. The game clock, which is not yet running, starts only with the snap of the ball. It continues to run as normal play proceeds by the sequence of downs, and is stopped, if necessary and only momentarily, to allow for the officials to disentangle a pile of players before respotting the ball. Following this, both the game clock and the 30-second clock restart. If the quarterback overruns the 30-second clock, the game clock is stopped and the offending team is assessed a yardage penalty. The adjustment having been made, the 30-second clock restarts, but again the game clock restarts only when the ball is snapped. The game clock also stops when the ball or the ball-carrier goes out of bounds, and when a forward pass is dropped (incomplete). Again, after each of these events, the 30-second clock is started immediately the ball is respotted, but the game clock restarts only when the ball is snapped. Additionally, there are other occasions when it is reasonable that playing time should not be used up, such as when, following a change in possession, the existing on-field squads are replaced by their counterparts. A complete list is given in the Rules section.

Each team is given the option to stop the game clock (take a 'Time Out'), three times in each half, to allow the quarterback or defending team captain to discuss tactics with his coach. This privilege is, one must admit, abused, as a team will hold back its Time Outs and use them merely as a device for stopping the clock if losing late in the game.

Finally, and one suspects simply to allow for the emotional build-up to the grand finale, the game clock is stopped officially two minutes before the end of each half. It restarts when the ball is snapped to begin the final two minutes of play.

THE OFFICIALS

The standard dress for officials is shown in Fig 68. The referee is the only one who wears a black cap.

The Referee is the senior official and final arbiter in all matters concerning the rules of the game. He concentrates largely on the snap of the ball and the movements of the quarterback and running backs.

The Umpire observes the actions of offensive interior linemen.

The Head Linesman rules on the movement of players, at the line of scrimmage, immediately prior to the snap of the ball.

Fig 68: *An official*

END ZONE

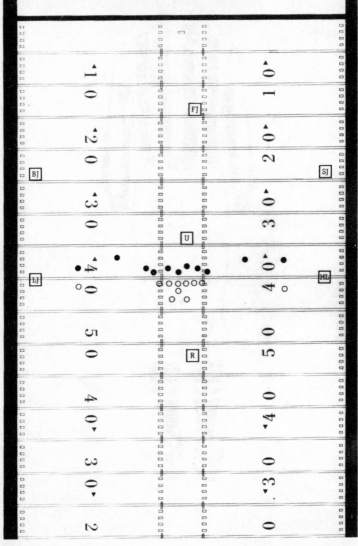

The Line Judge has similar responsibilities to those of the Head Linesman, but in addition he will observe the actions of receivers close to the line of scrimmage.

The Back Judge rules on matters concerning pass receptions, including any interference and the inbounds completion of a pass.

The Side Judge operates essentially as does the Back Judge, but in addition looks for illegalities in line play.

The Field Judge observes plays associated with the tight end.

Of course, all the officials have complete mastery of the rules, and can be consulted on those occasions when the official normally responsible for spotting infringements is unsighted. The positions which they adopt immediately prior to the snap of the ball, are shown in Fig 69.

Fig 69: *The positions of the officials prior to the snap of the ball*

CHAPTER X

OFFICIAL SIGNALS AND RULES

TOUCHDOWN (6 pts), EXTRA POINT (1 pt), FIELD GOAL (3 pts)

A **touchdown** would normally be scored by rushing or passing but there are other ways worth bearing in mind, as follows:

(a)   Following a fumble recovery or an interception by a defensive player, the ball can be advanced as a part of that very play.

(b)   On recovery of a blocked field goal attempt or punt, the ball can be advanced by players of either team.

(c)   By the direct return of a kick off or punt (this one is really spectacular).

The **extra point** is normally scored by a kick from a scrimmage on the 2-yard line. However, it is quite legal to run or pass the ball into the end zone, as for scoring a touchdown. Whatever the method used, the score is still only 1 point. By contrast, in College Football, a run or pass into the end zone is worth 2 points.

A **field goal** attempt can be made on any down, from any part of the field. If unsuccessful, possession is transferred to the opposition which begins its series of downs at the point of the line of scrimmage from which the attempt was made. Following an unsuccessful attempt which was from a point inside the opposition 20-yard line, play restarts at the 20-yard line.

SAFETY (2 points concession to the opposition)

A player, in full possession of the ball, is trapped within *his* end zone or is forced to run out of *his* end zone in any direction other than the forward direction. It applies *only* when the man in possession has entered the end zone under his own impetus, in other words, he has entered the end zone either by choice or obligation, but under his own steam. When a player in possession has been tackled in the end zone under the following circumstances, a safety is *not* conceded but rather, play restarts with a 1st down on the 20-yard line:

(a) A player *already in the end zone* gathers a punt, a kick off, or makes either an interception or a fumble recovery.

(b) A player gathers the ball, e.g. makes an interception, and falls into the end zone as part of that act.

FIRST DOWN

From four or fewer downs, 10 or more yards have been gained, thus earning for the offense another series of four downs.

LOSS OF DOWN

This signal indicates a loss of down associated with a penalty, or loss of down resulting from an incomplete forward pass.

DEAD BALL or NEUTRAL ZONE ESTABLISHED

This signals that the ball has been respotted in position for the next down and that the 30-second clock should be started. This 30 seconds is the time allowed for the offense to initiate the next play.

TIME OUT

An official on the field, or the official time keeper, will stop the game clock under the following circumstances:

(a)   At the request for a time out by the captain of either team. Three time outs are allowed per team in each half.

(b)   Two minutes before the end of each half.

(c)   Following a score.

(d)   Following an infringement of the rules.

(e)   Following a change in possession and the consequences of that, e.g. a return run.

(f)   When a fair catch is signalled and made.

(g)   When a forward pass is incomplete.

(h)   When a player is injured.

(i)   When the ball goes over the side line.

(j)   When necessary to unpile the players in order to re-spot the ball.

Two important consequences of the rules governing timing are listed below:

(a)   A team in the lead and close to the end of normal time, will attempt to keep the clock running by using only rushing plays and in so doing, keep the ball within bounds and avoid stopping the clock by say, an incomplete pass. This is known as 'ball control'.

(b)   A team losing and with time running out, will ignore rushing plays in favour of passes down the side lines. On completion of a pass, the receiver will hop over the side line, thus stopping the clock. Even should the pass go to ground (be incomplete), the clock will be stopped. This tactic, which will occur either in or close to the final two minutes of a half, is known as 'the two minute drill'.

TIME IN or RESTART THE GAME CLOCK WHEN THE WHISTLE BLOWS

This indicates that the game clock must continue to run after the following events which may lead to doubt for the official time-keeper.

(a)   When a play (rushing or passing) has terminated, close to the side line but still in bounds.

(b)   After the brief pause to allow for re-spotting the ball, if necessary, and signalled by a whistle.

PENALTY REFUSED, INCOMPLETE PASS, PLAY OVER, MISSED FIELD GOAL

Penalty refused: There are occasions when it would be to the disadvantage of the defense to enforce a penalty on the offense. In these cases, the penalty option is declined by the defensive captain. For example, a penalty by the offense on 4th down, with the retention of down, would give the offense another bite at the cherry. If, on the play which had incurred the penalty, the offense had not reached the ten-yard marker, the ball would automatically be transferred to the defense, and this is of greater value than would be any yardage penalty.

Incomplete pass: A forward pass is dropped or goes out of bounds.

Play over: Play from a particular down has ended.

Missed field goal: A field goal attempt is unsuccessful.

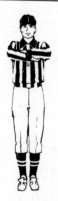

DELAY OF GAME

This occurs when the quarterback overruns the 30 second clock (takes more than 30 seconds to begin the next play). The offense is charged a 5-yard penalty with no loss of down. For example, following this infringement on 2nd and 10, initially on the offense 30-yard line, the succeeding down would be 2nd and 15 on the offense 25-yard line.

Very rarely, a team will delay the kick off at the beginning of a half, or restarting after a score. There could be two examples of this. (Note that a kick off will normally take place from the kicking team's 35-yard line.)

(a)   A team is on the field but, in a slovenly manner, simply takes too much time (over 30 seconds). The kick must be retaken from the kicking team's 30-yard line.

(b)   If the team is not on the field in reasonable time to start the game (disgraceful), the same distance penalty is assessed but in addition, the kicking team loses its coin toss options. The team which otherwise would be receiving the kicked ball, assumes the right to the options.

ILLEGAL MOTION

One offensive strike player (eligible receiver) may be 'in motion', running behind and parallel to the line of scrimmage during the starting count. However, he must not turn upfield before the ball is snapped. The penalty is a loss of five yards but retention of down.

OFFSIDE or ENCROACHMENT

This occurs in both offensive and defensive line play. Essentially, linemen of either team may not be in or cross the neutral zone (the no man's land in between the two lines) at the moment the ball is snapped. Whilst offensive players must be motionless, those on defense may enter the neutral zone momentarily, before the snap, but are not allowed to contact the offensive players and, after entering, must immediately withdraw.

For both offensive and defensive violation, the penalty is a loss of five yards but no loss of down (offensive).

FALSE START or ILLEGAL FORMA-TION

This is associated with offensive line play.

False start: Once having assumed a set position (three point stance), a lineman may not prematurely lunge forward (prior to the snap).

Illegal formation: The offense must have at least seven men on the line of scrimmage, e.g. a wide receiver, five interior linemen and a tight end would suffice. To have fewer men is penalised under this heading.

For both violations, the penalty is loss of five yards but retention of down.

ILLEGAL FORWARD PASS

Only one forward pass is allowed, and it must be from behind the line of scrimmage.

(a)   For a second forward pass, the penalty is loss of down from the previous down position, e.g. a second forward pass from the offense 30-yard line during 2nd down and 10, would become 3rd down and 10 from the same 30-yard line.

(b)   A forward pass from beyond the line of scrimmage is penalised by loss of down *and* loss of 5 yards. 2nd down and 10 from the offense 30-yard line would become 3rd down and 15 from the offense 25-yard line.

INTENTIONAL GROUNDING

The passer deliberately throws the ball to ground (not within five yards of an eligible receiver) in an effort to avoid being sacked. The defense has the option to enforce either of two penalties:

(a) Loss of 10 yards *and* loss of down, e.g. 2nd and 10 from the offense 40-yard line would become 3rd and 20 from the offense 30-yard line.

(b) The ball may be respotted at the point from which the pass was thrown (perhaps inflicting an even greater loss of yardage) together with loss of down. If this alternative spot was in the end zone, a safety score (2 points) would be conceded by the offense.

PASS JUGGLED INBOUNDS, CAUGHT OUT OF BOUNDS

This concerns the validity of a pass reception. To be a completion, the ball must clearly be under the full control of the receiver who, if in isolation, must land with *both* feet in bounds (he must not touch the side line when making contact with the ground). However, the pass would be a legal completion were he to catch the ball in the air and yet, before touching down, be driven over the line by the momentum of the tackle, before he could land.

Failing these, the pass is incomplete and the penalty loss of down. From, say, 1st and 10 from the offense 50-yard line, the next play becomes 2nd and 10 from the same 50-yard line.

INELIGIBLE RECEIVER TOUCHES A FORWARD PASS

Only certain players are eligible pass receivers. These are those (two) players at the extreme ends of the front (offensive) line, together with those who, at the snap of the ball, are positioned more than one yard back from this front line (usually running backs and a flankerback). The penalty depends on the field location where the ball was touched:

On or behind the line: The penalty is loss of down at the previous spot. 2nd and 10 from the 30-yard line would become 3rd and 10 from the same 30-yard line.

Beyond the line: The penalty is loss of down (as above) *or* loss of 10 yards but retention of down (choice belongs to defense). In the second alternative, 2nd and 10 on the offense 30-yard line would become 2nd and 20 on the offense 20-yard line.

INELIGIBLE RECEIVER DOWN-FIELD

This is a violation associated with both passing and kicks from scrimmage (punts and field goal attempts).

Passing: On passing plays, ineligible receivers are not allowed to travel more than one yard beyond the line of scrimmage until the ball has left the passer's hand. The penalty is a loss of 10 yards with retention of down, e.g. 2nd down and 10 from the offense 30-yard line, becomes 2nd and 20 from the offense 20-yard line.

Punts: Only the two ends are allowed to travel beyond the line of scrimmage after the snap but before the ball is punted. Penalty for violation of this rule is a loss of five yards. 4th and 10 from the defense 40-yard line, would become 4th and 15 from the defense 45-yard line.

PASS INTERFERENCE

Once the ball has left the passer's hand, *no* player, either offensive of defensive, may make contact with another player such as would hinder the opportunity to catch the ball. Simultaneous and incidental contact, when making a genuine attempt to catch the ball, is allowed. Simply barging into a player to prevent his catching the ball is not allowed.

Interference by offensive player: The penalty is a loss of 10 yards from the previous line of scrimmage. 2nd and 10 from the offense 30-yard line, becomes 2nd and 20 from the offense 20-yard line.

Interference by defensive player: The offense is awarded a first down at the point of illegal contact. If this point is in the end zone, play would restart with a first down on the 1-yard line.

INVALID FAIR CATCH SIGNAL

When facing any kick, the player on the receiving team can signal 'fair catch' by holding up one arm whilst awaiting arrival of the ball. In attempting the catch, he must not be tackled. However, once having made the catch, he is not allowed to make a return run. The official would make the invalid fair catch signal if he was not satisfied with the kick receiver's indication of his intention to make a fair catch. In violation, the receiving team will start its return drive (1st down) from a point five yards deeper than the point of reception.

ILLEGAL USE OF HANDS, ARMS OR BODY

This rule is primarily concerned with blocking on both rushing and passing plays. In both cases, obstruction of an opponent by tackling him is not allowed.

Pass blocking (protection of the passer): The blocker may use his hands, open or closed, but not in the attempt to grasp. Any contact with an opponent must be on his frame only (not the neck, face or head). Furthermore, the blocker's hands must be *inside his elbows* (he is not allowed to spread his arms).

Run blocking (protection of the ball carrier on a rushing play, even in open field): The blocker can use the whole of the upper part of his body but must not use his extended arms.

In both cases, the penalty is the loss of ten yards but with retention of down. 2nd and 10 from the offense 30-yard line, becomes 2nd and 20 from the offense 20-yard line.

HOLDING

It is illegal to grasp hold of an opponent's shirt when protecting the ball carrier. For the defensive player, it is permissible to grasp an opponent's shirt in the attempt to wrestle him aside, but grasping his shirt in the attempt to prevent him leaving the scene to join in open play, is illegal. The penalties are:

Offensive holding: A ten-yard loss with retention of down.

Defensive holding: A five-yard loss and also an automatic first down to the offense.

TRIPPING

In protecting the runner, it is illegal to trip an opponent (flipping his legs by using hands or feet). The penalty is a loss of ten yards with retention of down.

CRAWLING, INTERLOCKING INTERFERENCE, PUSHING OR HELPING THE RUNNER

Crawling: This is the attempt by a runner who has been fairly downed to gain extra yardage by crawling along the ground. The penalty is a loss of five yards from the spot where he was officially downed, with retention of down.

Interlocking interference: In assisting the runner, his team mates are not allowed to interlock arms and thus form a protective wall. The penalty is a loss of ten yards but with retention of down.

Pushing or helping the runner: In assisting the runner, offensive players are not allowed to add their weight to his forward momentum (i.e. by giving him a shove). The penalty is a loss of ten yards with retention of down.

BALL ILLEGALLY KICKED OR BATTED

Kicking: The ball, in open play, must not be fly-kicked, as might happen in rugby.

Batting: The ball in the possession of a runner may not be batted out of his grasp, nor, if it is bouncing around the field, may it be batted in a forward direction.

The penalty, for a guilty defense, is an automatic 1st down to the offense. For a guilty offense, it is a loss of fifteen yards with retention of down.

ILLEGAL CONTACT

A defensive player (usually a defensive back) may not impede an eligible pass receiver, running his pass pattern, once the receiver has proceeded more than five yards beyond the line of scrimmage. The penalty is a loss of five yards, measured from the original line of scrimmage, and an automatic first down to the offense.

ILLEGAL BLOCKING BELOW THE WAIST

No player on the receiving team is allowed to block below the waist while the ball is in the air from a kick or punt, or while assisting the kick or punt returner in his upfield run. This is a personal foul (see later) and the penalty is a loss of fifteen yards from the point of the illegal block.

ILLEGAL CRACKBACK BLOCK

This is a restriction against blocking below the waist by a player who lines up more than two yards outside the limits of the interior line, or is an eligible receiver in the backfield. Any contact with an opponent who is trying to reach the ball must be above the opponent's waist and *not* from the rear. The penalty is a loss of fifteen yards but the down is retained.

PERSONAL FOUL

Several acts of horror are included under the heading of personal foul. In each case, the penalty is the loss of fifteen yards, and for a guilty defense, the additional award of a first down to the offense.

Striking, kicking or kneeing: These are classed as physical assault.

Grasping the face mask: This is the dangerous act of using an opponent's face mask to twist his head. However, for non-violent contact with a face mask the penalty is reduced to a loss of only five yards and an automatic first down in the case of a guilty defense.

Roughing the kicker or passer: This is unnecessary contact after the ball has been kicked or passed.

Roughing the runner: This is the act of tackling the runner when he is clearly down or out of bounds.

Piling on: Usually reserved for star running backs, this treatment involves several defensive players adding their weight to the initial tackle, once the runner is down.

Clipping: This is a block performed from the rear and below the waist. It is particularly dangerous (see below).

UNSPORTSMANLIKE CONDUCT

This is equivalent to what is known as 'ungentlemanly conduct' in some sports, and

is recognised by various names in most sports. Typically, it would include the use of foul and abusive language, persistent violation of the rules and generally being a bad sport. The penalty is a loss of fifteen yards with retention of down.

PLAYER DISQUALIFIED

For acts of unqualified violence and total disregard of authority, the player is sent off for the remainder of the game. He may be replaced quite legally by another player, which means that his team suffers the penalty only of not having one particular player available to play.

CHAPTER XI

FOOTBALL TERMINOLOGY

Audible: The signals called out by the quarterback when, at the line of scrimmage, he needs to alter the type of play.

Blitz: A defensive play designed to tackle the quarterback before he can deliver the pass. Usually, linebackers and a safety join in the pass rush. It is a risky play since it exposes the weakened backfield to the passing play if the quarterback can evade the blitz.

Blocking: Deliberately and legally obstructing an opposing player. The blocker is restricted as follows:

(a) he is not allowed to use hands to grab or hold

(b) he is not allowed to use arms to encircle or trip

(c) the block must be from a frontal direction

Blocking is to be distinguished from tackling (allowed only on the man with the ball) for which the only restrictions are those associated with the risk of serious injury, e.g. grabbing an opponent's face mask.

Chain crew: The officials, on the sidelines, who operate a ten-yard measuring chain. If there is a dispute over the yardage gained, the ten-yard chain is brought on and becomes the official measure of the yardage.

Clipping: A form of blocking by contacting an opponent from the rear and below the waist. It is an illegal act unless the action takes place as part of the defensive-offensive line interaction.

Completion: To catch a forward pass.

Cut: A sidestep when running at speed.

Delay of game: The quarterback fails to initiate play within the allowed 30 seconds.

Direct snap: The action of the offensive center who, at the start of the down, passes the ball backwards and some 5–7 yards to a teamate, e.g.

(a) the quarterback in the shotgun formation

(b) the holder for a conversion or field goal attempt

(c) the punter.

Dogging: An alternative name for blitzing.

Encroachment: Making contact with an opposing player before the ball is snapped. This usually means that a lineman has wrongly anticipated the snap of the ball and has lunged forward.

Fake: A quarterback pretends to do something in order to confuse the defense. He will 'fake' the hand off to a running back before passing to a receiver.

Flag on the play: The official throws down a yellow handkerchief during play to indicate that an offence has taken place.

Fumble: The ball is dropped by a player who previously had full control. This can be accidental or as the result of a tackle.

Goal line: The chalk line which marks the beginning of the end zone and separates it from the field of play.

Handoff: The smooth transfer of the ball by the quarterback, usually to a running back.

Hang time: The flight time of a punted ball.

Hashmarks: The lines marking the central strip of playing area, and stretching the length of the field. All formal plays begin within or on the edge of this strip.

Huddle: The grouping of offensive players, having the next play explained, usually by the quarterback.

Incompletion: A forward pass is not caught within bounds.

Ineligible receiver: The offensive player, usually a lineman, who is not allowed to catch a forward pass.

Ineligible receiver downfield: The ineligible receiver who has moved more than one yard beyond the line of scrimmage on a passing play, before the ball is passed.

Incompletion: A forward pass that is not caught within bounds.

In motion: An offensive player who, before the snap of the ball, moves to another starting position is said to be in motion. He must run laterally, and is allowed to change direction and turn upfield only after the snap.

Intentional grounding: A pass deliberately thrown to ground by the quarterback, to avoid being tackled in possession for a loss of yards.

Interference block: The travelling block by a player leading the ball-carrier.

Interior lineman: The five players, tackles, guards and center, who form the interior of the offensive line.

Knuckle ball: This is a term borrowed from baseball and used to describe the motion of the ball in flight. Instead of gently rotating about its axis, it tumbles.

Lateral pass: The pass in a sideways or backward direction (as in rugby).

Line drive: A term borrowed from baseball and used to describe a ball which is kicked with great force and which travels a distance, essentially parallel with the ground.

Lineman: A player who forms part of the front line, either offensive or defensive, at the start of a down.

Line of scrimmage: The imaginary line which passes through the ball from sideline to sideline and across which the opposing linemen face each other in their formal down positions.

Measuring chain: The official measure of yardage gained. See also under Chain crew.

Neutral zone: The 11-inch strip of ground, the length of the football, stretching laterally from sideline to sideline and straddling the line of scrimmage.

Offensive holding: The illegal use of hands by an offensive player in grabbing or holding an opponent.

Offside: A lineman, either offensive or defensive, beyond the line of scrimmage when the ball is snapped, is offside.

Onside kick: The short kick off, as the alternative to the more usual long kick off, following a score, used when the kicking team desperately needs to regain possession to score again.

Pass interference: Illegal contact made by either player in the attempt to catch or intercept a forward pass.

Penalty marker: The yellow flag (handkerchief) thrown by an official, whilst play is in progress, to indicate that an offence has taken place.

Personal foul: An act of violent contact outside the rules of the game, e.g. clipping, late tackle, kicking or punching.

Piling on: The unnecessary adding of players' weight to the tackles of others, once the ball-carrier is clearly downed.

Pitchout: As an alternative to the handoff, when the quarterback tosses the ball laterally to a running back.

Play action: The motion of a quarterback to one side or the other, as a prelude to delivering his pass. As an alternative, he might stand firm in the pass protection pocket.

Pocket: The protected area from inside which the quarterback delivers his pass.

Prevent defense: The deliberate reinforcement of the defensive backfield to amplify the defense against the expected long pass.

Punt return: The distance of the runback following a successful reception of the punted ball.

Roughing the kicker: The deliberate, forceful and illegal contact with the kicker after he has kicked the ball away.

Roughing the passer: Similar to roughing the kicker, but in this case, the illegal contact is with the passer after he has delivered his pass.

Rushing play: Running with the ball following a handoff, pitchout or lateral pass.

Sack: To tackle the quarterback in possession of the ball behind the line of scrimmage, for a loss of yards.

Side line: Similar to the touchline of soccer and rugby. As in the case of rugby, but not soccer, the sideline is out of bounds.

Shift: The concerted movement of offensive players in adjusting to a new alignment immediately prior to the snap of the ball.

Snap: The transfer of the ball from the center to the quarterback, initiating play at the line of scrimmage. The center, standing with his legs astride, passes the ball back through his legs.

Spearing: The act of diving at a player, helmet first, when he is already clearly grounded.

Stunting: The act of an outside linebacker who loops round an inside linebacker to penetrate the offensive line through its middle.

Tackling: The act of bringing down or clearly holding with one's arms the man with the ball. See under 'blocking' for the difference between tackling and blocking.

Time in: The game-clock is running.

Time out: The game-clock is stopped either at the request of the captain or as directed by the officials.

Touchback: The act of restarting play from the 20-yard line when, following a kick or punt, the ball has passed through the end zone or, having gathered the ball within the end zone, a defender declines any return run.

Two-minute warning: The automatic time out which occurs two minutes before the end of each half.

Unsportsmanlike conduct: Ungentlemanly conduct.

Yardage: A distance measured in yards.

TIPS FOR TELEVISION VIEWERS

Now that you've read this book, and know what the game is about, you might find the following tips helpful when watching television.

Watch the Quarterback As a start, rather than searching for the ball, focus on the quarterback, watching his movements. If he drops straight back he is going to pass, but if he rolls and fakes, you cannot be sure what he will do. Having got used to the fact that he will be floating around in the backfield, the man with all the options, you can start to take in the wider picture of things.

Try to Predict the Next Play On third down with more than five yards to go, a pass is almost certain. This will be strongly indicated if three wide receivers appear in the lineup. When only a short gain is needed, extra offensive linemen, more than seven on the line of scrimmage, will signal a running play.

Watch the Offensive Linemen On a pass play they are not allowed to smash down the field, so very rapidly they will all drop back to form a pocket for the quarterback, confirming the pass. If they all lunge forward, they are clearing the way for a running back.

Identify Linebackers and Safeties: Are They Coming or Going?
Defensive linemen will be bent over with one or both hands touching the ground. Linebackers and safeties will be crouched and hovering. If they rush forward, they are 'blitzing', i.e. trying to nail the quarterback. If they withdraw from the line action, they are almost certainly setting up a zone defensive pattern. There will

always be one linebacker, the real killer, who will go for the ball whatever and whoever is in the way.

Punting and Field Goal Attempts It is often more fun to watch the defensive players who will charge round the end of the offensive line, trying to block the kick.

Kickoff and Punt Receiving Anticipating the return run, it is best to focus in front of the punt/kickoff receiver, looking for lead blockers who are trying to establish a running lane to spring him into open field. Once there, he is going 'all the way'.

Time Out Keep a count of these (each team is allowed three in each half) because they are crucial when teams want to stop the clock towards the end of each half.

Sneaky Play Section

(a) A quarterback will drop back as if to pass but instead will hand the ball to a running back. This is the 'draw' play.

(b) The quarterback might toss the ball to a running back who then throws a forward pass. This is the 'half back option play' and is perfectly legal.

(c) Look for a short kickoff, the 'onside kick', near the end of a half.

(d) Punters, holders and kickers are perfectly entitled to run and pass just as for a formal down. It is perfectly legal, rather cunning, and a favourite trick down in Dallas.

Illustration Acknowledgement   The publishers wish to thank Michael Hodson Designs for creating the diagrams, and Gerry Malone for the illustrations which appear in this book.